Full Circle

Syed Kamil

Joyson Publishers—Westborough, MA
ISBN: 979-8-9857856-0-9
Library of Congress Control Number: 2022903663
Title: Full Circle
Author: Syed Kamil
Digital distribution | 2022
Paperback | 2022

Dedication

iii

To Adil
When he was a handsome young man with a beautiful
soul.

Introduction
Why a Book?

A window connecting East and West with interesting views for the curious.

I think I have lived an interesting, and varied life. During my life, I have learned a lot about myself and my fellow men that I hope some of you might find interesting, or perhaps even useful, as you continue your own journey through this thing, we call life. I have always wanted to write a book, and, really, what better way is there to share my experiences. In writing this book, I tried to do so without any bias or any inhibitions. I am convinced that every life has unique experiences and every person can contribute to the greater good of society by sharing their personal experiences. I think that truth has a certain charm that attracts readers who are curious. I have always been curious.

By profession, I am a surgeon, trained in Europe and the United States. I was born and raised in Peshawar, Pakistan, a city that has been at the center of political and religious strife throughout much of its history. I have spent my entire life negotiating cultural diversity and have been fortunate enough to have lived among people of many different cultures. My belief that a true understanding of life experiences can only be achieved by actual presence and interaction with people made me undertake this journey of self-reflection and soul searching. Practicing medicine in many different countries and being in close, personal contact with friends and patients has given me a unique insight. There is no doubt there are major differences between the East and the West and that these differences have been a source of many misunderstandings. Because I have lived in both cultures and have tried my best to understand both sides, I am hoping to give the readers my insights into how we can learn from some of these misunderstandings and make changes to prevent them from happening again.

We should be grateful and admire anyone who is trying to seek the truth, make sense of it, and then share it with others. He or she needs to be appreciated and respected because finding and understanding the truth is the most important thing a human being can do. It is not an easy task. The most challenging part is trying to sort through all the lies, falsehood, innuendo, and propaganda that surrounds one's life. Even then, some people choose to hold on to the truth so they can use it for personal gain.

With time our knowledge expands and our ability to comprehend and understand things becomes more polished. As we become more knowledgeable the truth becomes more apparent. So, to find the truth one has to be smart, educated, and have the desire to look for it. Through this book, I hope my experiences and insights will help others who are in pursuit of the truth; of looking at the whole picture. Perhaps my experiences can benefit society or even just one person. It is not important if my experiences are liked or disliked by readers, or whether or not they agree with some of my observations. I just hope my thoughts on life might give the readers something to think about without telling them what is right and what is wrong.

The premise of the book:

When cancer has been discovered in a body, people immediately look for the reason why or how cancer may have started. For example, cancers can be caused by environmental factors such as pollution or exposure to UV light. They can also be caused by lifestyle or behavioral choices such as smoking, poor nutrition, or a lack of physical activity. Education also plays a part. If people aren't aware of the risks, or if there is apathy, then it is harder to stay healthy. Sometimes, before a diagnosis has been made, one might ignore the warning signs of cancer or they might deny that cancer is even a possibility. If cancer is ignored, left untreated, or treated improperly, it will eventually spread throughout the body and the person will die.

Much the same can be said about society. The same factors that can cause cancer in humans, can also be related to the destruction of society as well. There are environmental, behavioral, and educational factors that can lead to societal fragility. And just like cancers in humans, if ignored, left untreated, or worse, encouraged, societal problems/influencers will grow, spread and eventually lead to the destruction of society. Of course, it is not all bad news. Throughout the course of history, society has not only survived but has also grown and flourished and thrived.

In the following chapters, I will try to show you examples from my life in which I think society has both failed and succeeded in its treatment of "societal cancers". Along the way, I will give some suggestions as to how we might be able to do better.

I first started thinking about this when I had the sad experience of telling a young man that he had cancer… I will tell you more about him later. But first, let me tell you a bit about my childhood.

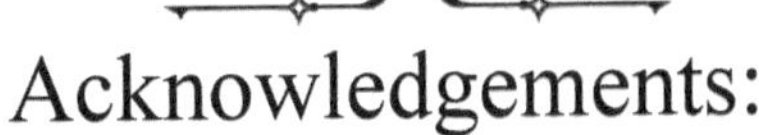

Acknowledgements:

I wish to express my gratitude to my wife and children who have been a source of great pleasure in my life and have provided me with the inspiration to write this book.
I would also like to thank Caroline Rider who helped me with editing and Em Hughes who helped me with publishing.

Chapter 1
Where it All Started

We were sitting outside in Qissa Khawani, the Street of the Storytellers, the most famous bazaar in Peshawar. We were close to the Khyber Pass, the gateway to India and Pakistan from Afghanistan. It was here that merchants traveling along the old Silk Road would gather to conduct their business and exchange stories from their travels. On this day, as we waited for our food to arrive, it seemed as chaotic and vibrant as it must have been hundreds and even thousands of years ago.

I was aware of the significance of this place, so filled with dust and smoke. So loud with traffic noise. I imagined the interactions of ancient travelers from China, Central Asia, and Europe. How they slept in the old hotels or enjoyed meals with their friends, as we were doing now. I saw myself going through the same cycle of life as they had and could not help but think about how this place would be here long after I was gone. Who would sit there in a few hundred years? Which, if any, of my descendants?

We sat at an old table along the side of the road and had to shout to be heard. But we had all grown up in this part of the world and were used to the chaos. With our eyes, we followed old trucks, battered cars, scooters, motorcycles with no mufflers, horse-drawn tongas, and three-wheeled motorized rickshaws that often toppled sideways and always left their passengers at the mercy of the driver. We watched roadside vendors push their four-wheeled carriages to and from their homes, and shoppers buying perfume, jewelry, shoes, and cigarettes. We saw the sick visit dentists as well as quacks who boasted the ability to treat any illness — toothaches, epilepsy, erectile dysfunction — with an elixir of youth and power. In this most conservative part of Pakistan, most of the passersby were men, but occasionally we saw women in burqas, their eyes visible through small holes in their shawls.

Many restaurants in this area were owned by Afghan refugees and I craved pulao rice and chickpeas. But some Pakistanis would not eat in those restaurants because they believed the refugees took business away from natives in Peshawar, so we chose a local restaurant that displayed different types of meat on sticks. We selected a leg of lamb, which was carried to an open-air coal oven just a few feet from where we sat. While we waited, the waiter offered us a joint, a common practice that whetted our appetites before the meal.

We talked about school, friends, girls, and politics, jumping from topic to topic. Each of us was studying medicine but we had plenty of free time because we were living in a country that had banned alcohol and bars and most music concerts. So this is how we spent our time, in conversation in restaurants, in public bazaars.

One of the most common topics of discussion at that time was the Russian invasion of Afghanistan, which had sent two million Afghans fleeing their homes to settle in Peshawar during the war. A few of my friends had already joined the fight against the Russians and had returned to describe their experiences. My friend Kamran would talk in great detail about his feeling of fulfillment as he fought alongside the Taliban and defeated the Russians during one of their encounters.

The people living along the border between Afghanistan and Pakistan shared common social and cultural values. They spoke the same language of Pashto. The invasion of Afghanistan was basically an invasion into their own territory, and deeply religious Pakistanis, like Kamran, believed they had a duty to beat back the Russians. We would listen to him list the duties of every Muslim, but none of us cared - I had no interest or intention of joining the fight — and he knew that very well.

My other friend Hamza quietly smoked cigarettes during our conversation. From time to time he would smile to show that he was listening, inhaling the smoke deeply into his lungs before blowing it out. He was well built, handsome and clean-shaven, dressed in pants and a shirt, a westernized style he adopted after years at a private boarding school. He seemed to be the most content among us, with no intention of confronting anyone's religious beliefs or any other controversial subjects for that matter. He only wanted to have a good time.

We all had different expectations and different future plans. Kamran wanted to pursue the religious path, but deep inside him was confusion. Hamza was content to blow with the wind. I wanted to follow the sun, to rise in the East and travel to the West. Maybe that was how my ancestors felt when they left their homeland and migrated to India, probably from Iran. I wanted to leave Pakistan. In my heart, I was sure this was not the place where I wanted to spend my whole life. I knew that sooner or later I would travel and discover a place that suited me better.

As we talked, we saw the blast. A bus in the distance lit up; a fiery explosion. We knew what had happened immediately.

This was a common occurrence in Qissa Khawani. Every few weeks there would be some kind of terrorist attack related to the war in Afghanistan, an explosion resulting in the loss of innocent life. No one ever knew who was behind these attacks. Some said that Russia was trying to teach the Pakistani government a lesson since Pakistan and America were working together to defeat the Russians. Some blamed it on the Taliban. Some blamed the CIA.

This particular bomb went off very close to where we sat, and the panic was immediate. But as the rest of us were running away from the explosion, Hamza did the opposite; he ran straight toward the bus. The next thing I knew, he was carrying a little girl in his arms. She was bleeding profusely. He stopped a rickshaw and directed the driver to take them to the nearest hospital which was about a mile down the road. Other help would have arrived too late.

A lot of people died that day, and many were seriously injured. But we learned later that the girl Hamza carried away had survived.

And that was how our evening ended — not a very unusual end in the Peshawar of my youth.

Chapter 2
The Hippy Trail

Peshawar's fascinating history stretches back to Alexander the Great. His army conquered Gandhara, the ancient name for the city and kingdom of Peshawar, in 327 BC, leaving behind clear genetic evidence of its occupation in the form of the many blue-eyed, blond-haired people. Persians, Aryans, Mongols, and later the Mughals in the seventeenth century also wandered through its antiquated streets. It is located on the edge of the Khyber Pass near the Afghan border. The Khyber Pass is a mountain pass connecting Afghanistan and Pakistan. It is an integral part of the ancient Silk Road and is one of the oldest known passes in the world. Throughout history, it has been an important trade route between Central Asia and the Indian Subcontinent. For centuries, it was the target of successive Afghan, Persian, and Mongol invaders. A personal residence of the Afghan Durrani rulers, Peshawar was taken by the Sikhs, from whom the British captured it in 1848. During the decade-long Soviet occupation of Afghanistan (1979–1989), it was the command center of the coalition of guerrilla groups intent on expelling the Soviet forces from Afghanistan. More recently, Peshawar and the surrounding area have been the scene of Taliban activity and attacks.

Peshawar was one of the major trade cities on the old Silk Road. The route stretched from China to the Mediterranean. This was the route that most westerners took to see the beautiful and varied parts of the world. It was a window into thousands of years of ancient civilizations. In ancient times the Silk Road was full of surprises. There were many delights and treats from many different people, countries, and cultures. Restaurants served all types of food and shops sold strange and wonderful surprises. Along the route, there were cities and small towns where the caravans of travelers camped and intermingled with other merchants and travelers.

Like many of these places, Peshawar, linked the civilizations of Europe and Asia via Iran, across the mountains of Afghanistan, over the Khyber Pass, and into the valley of Pakistan. Much later this route became known as the "Hippy Trail" due to the overland journey that was taken by members of the hippie subculture in the mid-twentieth century. The interaction between westerners and the local people, who dressed differently, spoke differently and had different customs, was a delight and an adventure to the people who ventured across the Hippy Trail.

As I was growing up in that vibrant city I watched lots of foreign tourists coming and going into the mountains or following the routes toward India. Their journeys would typically start from cities in western Europe, often London, Copenhagen, West Berlin, Paris, Amsterdam, or Milan. Most journeys passed through Istanbul, where the routes divided. The typical northern route passed through Tehran, Herat, Kandahar, Kabul, Peshawar, and Lahore onto India,

Nepal, and Southeast Asia. An alternate route was from Turkey via Syria, Jordan, and Iraq to Iran and Pakistan. Tourists would spend much of their time in this ancient city browsing around, smoking weed, and meeting with the locals. I remember the train station, which was not far from my house. It was always full of backpackers who were sleeping on the ground while waiting to catch the next train to wherever. It was a relatively peaceful time.

The atmosphere and hospitality of the locals, the winding streets of the town, and the ancient markets selling all sorts of souvenirs such as shawls, carpets, artwork, jewelry, and gemstones, attracted everyone. It was a city of tolerance, openness, and a place where foreigners felt welcome and safe. As a child, I would see them with their backpacks and would dream of traveling and exploring the world like they were doing. I took any opportunity that I could to ask them about their home countries, their cultures, and their experiences.

Everything started to change when the Russians invaded Afghanistan. With their invasion, religious fervor started to take hold, and the Taliban's existence came into being. The Taliban began to galvanize the locals to fight against the Russians. Their motivation was to take their country back and to start a jihad against the Russians who were non-Muslims occupying a Muslim nation. As the war was going on in Afghanistan, the refugees started to pour into Peshawar. Thousands came into the city. The city began to change not because of the refugees but because of the war in Afghanistan. The locals shared the same religion, language, and culture as the

Afghan people. Some of them even started to go and fight against the Russians in Afghanistan. The religious fanatics found the opportunity to stir up hatred against non-Muslims. The foreigners who used to be welcome now gradually started to feel unsafe and unwelcome in this city. Slowly the city, which was a pathway for all types of people for thousands of years, began to close its borders.

Ever since I became a father my dream has been to travel the Silk Road/Hippie Trail with my three children. However, circumstances beyond my control have made that dream a near impossibility, at least for the near future. The old Silk Road route has disappeared, not because it faded with time but because we humans have made it disappear. We were supposed to protect and improve this magical path to the far-flung cultures of the world for all future generations. Instead, people with wrong intentions have pushed religious fanaticism, political divisions, and local conflicts that have only been further intensified and inflamed by other outside powers hoping to gain some sort of control in the area. All of this has led to chaos and destruction in the region and beyond.

It is unfortunate that I, and my children, as well as countless other travelers, may never be able to travel through those paths. It is sad that we might never be able to experience the delights and surprises and adventures that were experienced by generations before us. We may never roam the bazaars of Baghdad or the beautiful gardens of Damascus. We may not experience the treats in Tehran or see the beautiful architecture in Isfahan. We may never experience the route through the Himalayan Mountains and travel through the Khyber Pass into the charming city of Peshawar. This should be the birthright of my children - to travel in the footsteps of their ancestors. All these beautiful and mysterious places that were so welcoming to locals and visitors alike are now death traps. The old hotels and restaurants have been taken over by religious fanatics who want to stop any interaction with the westerners.

The war hawks are destroying the beautiful world that existed peacefully for centuries. Don't they realize that when you light a match, it can spread like wildfire? Don't they understand that conflict spreads; that they can't always be contained? The entire region including Pakistan, Iran, and the Middle East is in chaos, and the consequences are spreading into Europe and the Americas. We have seen the peace disappearing and being replaced by chaos and terrorist attacks.

Rulers can create barriers, borders, and fences but once these conflicts start, they are like cancer. They take out everything in their path, both locally and across the world. Westerners can't presume to be safe because they are far away. Sooner or later the chaos and destruction will spread to them. If we don't reject chaos and hate, our children and grandchildren will suffer the consequences. I am sad that the world we are creating is becoming more unstable, more unsafe, more chaotic, and more unpleasant. Although we have not created these conflicts or divisions, by our complacency and indifference we are responsible for adding fuel to the fire.

Chapter 3
Deeper Wounds

The Partition of India was the division of British India in 1947 into two independent countries: India and Pakistan. The two self-governing countries of Pakistan and India legally came into existence at midnight on August 15, 1947. The partition displaced over 14 million people along religious lines, creating an overwhelming refugee crisis in the newly constituted countries. There was large-scale violence, with an estimated loss of life between several hundred thousand and two million. The violent nature of the partition created an atmosphere of hostility and suspicion between India and Pakistan that plagues their relationship to this day.

That is what the British did to India (as well as to many other countries). They were far from alone in doing this. Over the course of human existence, many countries have invaded and/or colonized other countries. Those invasions and colonizations have tended to leave the invaded countries in a lot of turmoil. That is precisely what happened to India after the British rule ended.

My parents never wanted to talk about their lives in India. I presume that any discussion of their past lives made them feel sad and that they wanted to protect us from the suffering they endured during the partition. I was, however, able to learn some of our family history from my maternal grandfather.

My grandfather was born and raised in India. According to my mother, he had lived a good life in a nice, big house with apple and mango orchards. He was a well-educated teacher and religious scholar who had written many books explaining Shia customs and beliefs. He had traveled to Iran and Iraq and had seen more of the world than anyone else I knew.

I remember him sitting on his bed with his glasses on his forehead reading and writing all day. Sometimes he would ask me to refill his ink bottle for his old-fashioned nib pens, or bring him tobacco for the Huka he smoked constantly. When I knew him, he was in his early seventies — an old man with a white beard, wearing a white turban, and almost always smiling. He looked very content and peaceful. I never saw any sign of worry or anger on his face, which is surprising given the ordeal he went through after the partition.

Upon the partition of India, my grandfather decided to remain in India, but he continued to travel to Iran and Iraq. During one of those trips, he decided to also go to Pakistan to visit my mother in Peshawar. This was in 1949, two years after the partition. When he tried to return to India, he was stopped by border guards. His house and all his property were confiscated by the Hindu government, and what little remained was looted. Suddenly, as an old man, he had lost everything — his job, his home, his country, and he became dependent on my mother. After several attempts and many applications, he was finally granted a travel visa to go to India, but he was never allowed to return to his house or to retrieve anything of his belongings. As a child, this was all I knew about the devastating consequences of the partition — an event that determined so much in the lives of my grandparents and parents, and in my own life.

My family was not alone in their suffering in the immediate and awful devastation of the partition. Literally, thousands upon thousands of Indian and Pakistani families were impacted by this decision; many were decimated. In fact, the effects of the partition are still being felt today. There is currently a conflict regarding Kashmir, which is the disputed land located between India and Pakistan. Both countries claim this land as their own. The hate on both sides is intense, and the two countries have fought three wars over this land since 1947.

For most of the 73 years since the partition, Pakistan has been under military rule. Even when it has not been directly in control, it has kept everything under check. The majority of the government budget is spent on the army, presumably to prepare against any future wars between India and Pakistan. Both countries have nuclear powers and spend most of their budget on defense. Meanwhile, there is immense poverty in both countries. The people are being exploited on religious and nationalistic grounds. Corruption is rampant.

As a surgeon, I know that if a wound is deep, the healing is complicated and takes time to heal. Every layer of the wound or defect has to be repaired properly. The healing has to start from the deepest layer and work its way to the surface, otherwise, it all breaks down and never fully heals properly. The same is true for healing the wounds between these two rival countries. The healing has to begin at its core.

To heal the wounds between the two countries, all the different layers of religious, ethnic, and social divisions that cause anger and hate have to be addressed. The politicians have to stop the exploitation of the people for their own interests. They have to stop using religious and ethnic differences against each other.

My hope is that India and Pakistan, along with the neighboring countries of Bangladesh and Sri Lanka, can create a union (much like the European Union) in which they can work together to form a strong coalition. The Europeans learned from the two devastating world wars fought on their soil and formed a union to prevent it from happening again. I think if a system like that is established in Southeast Asia it can start to heal wounds both ancient and new. Each independent country could keep its own borders, languages, religions, and cultures, but remove the travel bans. The citizens could travel at will among each country which would, in turn, help to establish better social and economic bonds. If people are able to travel and visit other places they will learn that, as humans, we have far more in common than differences, but the differences we do have should be embraced rather than rejected. Imagine how great society could be if governments spent less money on defense for the preparation of war and more on education, health, culture, and civic infrastructure.

This can only happen if the population is educated and understands that they will not be exploited by their leaders for their personal gains.

Although my grandfather is long gone, I still carry him very close. In my heart, he is still very much alive, and in times of trouble or adversity, I remember that he taught me to be humble and grateful for what I have, and through his actions and his teachings, I learned that in the face of adversity, I should remain calm and never give up hope.

Chapter 4
My Arrival

S hia Muslims observe the tenth day of Muharram, known as Ashura, as the date of the massacre in Karbala when Imam Hussein, grandson of the Prophet Muhammad, was martyred. They attend memorial services called Majlis, and they organize public mourning processions and reenactments of the Battle of Karbala. They perform public flagellations, through which they mourn Hussein's death and express their regret that they were not present at the battle to save Hussein and his family. Some Shia Muslims take part in Ashura for atonement, believing that "a single tear shed for Hussein washes away a hundred sins."

I was born at nine o'clock at night on the sixteenth day of June, three days before Ashura. It was hot in that small, one-bedroom house. The kitchen was a tiny closet. The house was stuffy, and the air was damp. There was no air-conditioning, only a fan. Stray dogs could be heard barking in the street outside. My father was out of the house, participating in the Majlis. But my mother had been through childbirth three times before with my two older brothers and a sister. She sent for Dai, an old Christian woman who had helped her during the birth of my siblings. There had been no visits to a doctor prior to my arrival, no prenatal examinations, no tests of any kind. With so little medical attention, it was quite common for a baby or a mother in my neighborhood to die during labor, and most people accepted such tragedies as the will of God. They took comfort in the conclusion that death was not in their control, that it was destiny or "kismet." But by the will of God, and with Dai's assistance, my mother and I survived.

As a child, I would watch the Majlis rituals every year, as grownups hit their heads and pounded their chests with their hands. Sometimes they would even use small chains with sharp blades to whip their backs. People of all ages would participate. Even children as young as eight or nine would bleed. Adults would cry. I never did any of it. Maybe I was not brave enough.

It is ironic, therefore, that I would be subjected to great pain at such a young age. But one day, when I was about 5 years old, a bearded man wearing a black turban came to the house. He was wearing multiple rings with colored stones on his fingers holding a box in his hand usually carried by barbers. My older siblings started to whisper when he appeared, so my younger brother and I knew something unpleasant was about to take place. My father greeted the man and led him inside. Then I was brought into a room to join them. There were no warnings or explanations, but I knew at that moment what was about to happen. The man opened his box of sharp instruments and clamps. I cried and tried to run away. But it was of no use. He pulled me out from under the bed and my father held me down. Very quickly, the man cut the little skin tag on my penis. I remember intense pain, some bleeding, and a bandage, but no one offered any pain medications.

Normally, boys are circumcised at the time of their birth, before memories are formed but it did not happen in my case. My parents probably thought to have both me and my younger brother, who was one at the time, circumcised at the same time for the sake of convenience. After all these years, the memory is still very fresh in my mind. I wonder what effect it still has on me. I know that my parents did not have the deeper insight or understanding in regards to long-term consequences. They loved me very much but that's how things were back then.

Chapter 5
A Most Beautiful Gift

In everyone's life, there are people (and places) that have influenced their lives. In my family, the partition of India to form the country of Pakistan was a very important event, as it was for millions of other families. It took my parents away from their parents and forced them to recreate their lives in a new place. After the partition, my mother followed my father to Pakistan and they settled in Peshawar. This separation from their families has to have affected their lives and the way in which they raised their own family.

My father married my mother in India. It was an arranged marriage. He had studied at Aligarh University in India which was one of the best institutions in that part of the world at that time. He emigrated to Pakistan when my mother was pregnant with my eldest brother. According to her, my father faced a lot of difficulties in the newly established country. He eventually decided to work as a teacher. He was smart and he worked hard, so he was able to establish his reputation as one of the best teachers in Peshawar. He was soon promoted to principal of a government high school. During his time as the principal, his high school became the best public high school in the whole province.

At that time in our culture, fathers did not interact much with their young children. For men to hold and play with a young child was probably seen as a sign of weakness. Fathers were not supposed to show their emotions. I do not remember playing with my father. I assume he loved his children but I do not remember him showing this until he was very old. By working as hard as he could he did everything he could to provide for our needs, but I only remember a few hugs on some special occasions. He also often worked late so that he could make more money in order to educate us better, but as a result, we did not see him as much. Deep inside I know he was a loving man, but he never showed this, and I believe that he did not show it because he did not know *how* to show it.

In contradiction to my father's lack of physical affection, my mother showered us with love and affection and hugs and kisses. My mother nursed me until I was two years old. She told me that it was the longest she nursed any of her children. In those days, in that place, women stayed home. They did not attend school as young girls. Some, like my mother, were homeschooled. She could read and write, but otherwise, she spent her time taking care of her family. She was the complete opposite of my father.

I was fortunate to have a mother who always protected me from harm and filled my early life with so much affection. There was an exceptional bond between us. She gave me unconditional love. A mother's love is one of the most significant contributions to society. Special love from a mother creates a person's character and soul. A mother's love during childhood makes the child feel calm and content while going through life's uncertain times. Mothers give comfort and security to a child's restless and vulnerable soul. They also provide the physical touch of reassurance and protection that every child needs. In my culture, there is a saying, "If you are looking for heaven, you will find it under the feet of your mother." This is a remarkable appreciation of all mothers for what they do for their children, family, and society in general. Mother is the central pillar of a family.

Today's societies, by putting more economic and financial pressure on families, have made this role very difficult. The pleasure of love, hugs, and kisses has been substituted by toys, gifts, and material things. These things can never replace the affection and attention of a loving mother. Societies should be grateful and should have a special appreciation for mothers who provide this vital gift that stays with us for the rest of our lives. This gift of pure and unconditional love cannot be bought. As a parent myself, I have come to realize how important it is for parents to hold and hug their children and give them comfort, not just with words or material things, but with physical contact. As the traumas and scars of childhood stay with us for the rest of our lives, similarly, the affection, love, and devotion that our mothers and families provided also stay with us forever.

I believe that by hugging and kissing loved ones, you share the deeper chemistry of your soul with their souls which develops a special memory deep in their minds. Your energy is shared with their energy. Your pleasure multiplies as you share their pleasure. I know that hugging and giving a physical touch to a grieving being lessens their pain. I know that by sincere physical contact you are diluting their pain as some of their pain comes into your body.

The comfort and love in the relationship between parents and their children who have experienced this type of bond can easily be seen by others. These families are happy and comfortable around each other and their physical bodies seem in harmony. I did not have this type of bond with my father. I know that he realized this when he was old. But sometimes things are learned too late; time passes and certain mistakes become irreversible. My father tried to hug me during the last two or three times I saw him. He would go out of his way to hold my hand. I could feel the tightness in his body. I knew he wanted to turn the clock back, but it was too late. My body was also tense on those occasions. It was not that we did not love each other, but neither of us was able to show our love for each other in a physical way. That made me realize that there is a critical period between kids and their parents when that bond happens and once that period has passed, it becomes very difficult to recreate that emotion, feeling, or affection.

As I grow older, reflecting on my life has become more exciting and meaningful. I start to analyze things more deeply, more critically and begin to think of all the people who have helped me become what I am today. I wonder about today's youth and what happens if they become restless, angry, harmful, or destructive. My hope is that the love and comfort that that person received as a child from a caring family could remind him or her to control that negative temptation. The anger and violence that is so rampant in our society today can be blamed partly on broken families where children crave love and security from their parents and family. More and more children are growing up in homes that lack affection and security and are looking for someone to nurture them. Luckily for me, I had my mother, and now my children have me to teach them about love.

Chapter 6
My Childhood Pleasures

For children in Peshawar, time often stood still. We had no activities after school. There were no clubs, no sports, no shared hobbies, and no organized activities. The days were long and there was very little entertainment except for the performers who visited our street from time to time.

Sometimes that was all we needed. We would wait to hear the song of the monkey trainer as he approached our section of the city. He was a grey-haired man, rather small in height but full of energy. He walked with a limp holding a cane in one of his hands. With his other hand, he led two Bandar monkeys, known for their mischievous behavior. Now that I think about it, he may have been from the part of India where monkeys are a common sight living among local people. These monkeys would be dressed as children, one a boy and one a girl. The girl would wear earrings and a lovely, colorful top. The boy wore a tie and shorts. They would ride on the trainer's shoulders, jumping from one shoulder to the other. They would run around him chasing each other, or sit on the ground and perform tricks. The boy would hold the girl's hand, hug her, or even sneak up behind her and pinch her. They would also imitate the trainer, copying the way he threw his hat, or mirror the children in the audience as they rubbed their heads or raised their hands.

The final act was always the highlight, as the monkeys collected objects that we brought from home as payment. Some would have fruit, others bread, and a few would bring toys. I usually would bring a few bunches of grapes from the grapevine in our backyard. I enjoyed feeding the monkeys right from my hand. The monkeys would approach each of us and take our offerings back to the trainer. We found this so exciting that we would always want to give them more. It was as if the monkeys realized that the children enjoyed their company and that they enjoyed the company of the children too. As we laughed harder, the monkeys became even more animated. Sometimes I wondered which of us was more delighted by the show.

Like the monkey trainer, the snake charmer also played a song to call us into the street. He would be playing the tune of a famous Bollywood song to attract the attention of the people. I can still hear his pipes in the distance. He was a small, older man in his fifties, with a beard, and he wore a turban on his head. He was a Hindu by religion. Hindus were in a minority in our part of the world but were known to respect all living forms of life, especially animals. On his turban, he carried three or four different baskets stacked on top of each other. We all knew what was inside.

It was mesmerizing to hear this man play his pipe —the distinct tune, and rhythm of a very old and popular Indian song. He would sit cross-legged on the ground in front of the closed basket, remove the lid and then start playing the flute. As the crowd focused on his music, he would open the lid of the smallest basket. Inside lay a black, coiled Viper with long hinged fangs. It would lay still for a moment as it got used to its surroundings, and then it would uncoil and lift its head. The crowd would hush with excitement. The man would bring his pipe closer to the snake and begin to sway in a rhythmic motion just in front of the snake's head. Slowly, the snake's head would begin to sway from side to side, as if it were completely controlled by the man's pipe. Crowd would gasp with fear and excitement along with the pleasure of the music. It was as if the snake charmer had hypnotized both the crowd and the snake at the same time.

The act would go on for a while. As the snake charmer slowed the movement of his pipe, lowered the tone of his song, and then dipped the pipe down, the snake would curl back into its basket. The man would then repeat the act with other snakes of different types and sizes. The final dancer was always a black cobra, with a beautiful multicolor pattern, which was easily five or six feet long. The man would begin to play his song and the cobra would rise. Its tongue would flick from its mouth and sometimes it would show its lethal fangs, but it was completely controlled by the small man and his pipe. Who could believe that something so strong and dangerous would submit to someone who appeared so weak? No matter how many times we watched this particular show (the snake charmer came around often) it always left us in a state of strange, heightened emotion with a mixture of anxiety, surprise and wonder.

But my favorite street performer of all was the dancing bear. The bear's trainer was a very old and wrinkled man, with a grey beard, wearing earrings and garlands of beads around his neck but he could command an animal more than ten times his size. He led the massive black bear which weighed about three hundred pounds with a brown V-shaped patch on the chest with a chain around its neck but the chain was only a prop to help the audience feel safe. There was no way this old man could control such a large creature with a thin chain.

They would arrive every few weeks to the sound of the old man's dug dugi, a small drum with two beads attached at the end of shorts strings, that pounded the drumheads when the drum was swung. The dugdugi can be heard from far away and we would run out as soon as we heard it. We would follow the old man and the bear until they found a suitable open space for their show. Then we would sit in a circle around the man and bear, perhaps too close in hindsight. We were very naïve. If we realized how strong the animal was, we would not have dared to sit a few feet away. But none of us understood the dangers as the old man told the bear to dance, jump, and rollover. It licked our hands and accepted any treats we might offer. After about thirty minutes, we would give the old man coins, food, even clothes as payment. It is amazing to me now that no one seemed to care that this huge, strong animal was performing in the middle of a crowded street.

I heard many rumors about the old man. Some said he was from far away. Some said he used to live in the high mountains of the Hindu Kush or the

Himalayas. Some said the old man found the bear when it was a very sick cub after its mother had abandoned it near the old man's house. They said he raised the bear like his own child since he seemed to have no children of his own. I still remember the affection they had for each other, how the bear would protect the old man as a son might protect a father.

After the show, we would follow them for some distance just to see where they were going. They looked like two friends enjoying each other's company as if they understood each other and never wanted to be apart. I knew the bear could have run away if it wanted to, or harmed the man. But it never did. It seemed to me that the bear knew it was keeping the old man alive by providing him with a livelihood and companionship. They seemed like a little family of two.

Chapter 7
Early Battles

The street performers were not the only animals in the lives of Peshawar children. As a young boy, I had rabbits, chickens, and pigeons as pets. It was the pigeons I enjoyed the most and always remember them with delight. My escape after a day at school was the company of my pet birds. They were my companions and I could not wait to see them.

I kept about twenty of them in small closets like cabins (where they sleep at night) on the roof of my house. My mother was not very happy about it because during the day the pigeons would sit around and poop all over the house. I did not care. They were my buddies. I knew each of them by their colors, their behavior, their actions. Some were loving, some were rebellious, some were brave, and some were more careful and cautious. They were all very smart. I could feel the happiness among them and within myself. I fed them and cared for them, and they gave me joy.

In the evenings I would go to the rooftop and fly my pigeons. I used a whistle to help guide and direct their flight. As I changed the tone, they would fly higher or lower, then circle the houses in wide or narrow arcs. Other people in the area also had pet pigeons and when they saw another group in the sky they would launch their own. Soon we would be engaged in a competition to decide whose birds were more loyal. This was a very common pastime. The groups would fly closer and closer until they intermingled. They would circle for a while until they were thoroughly mixed up. Then we blew our whistles to call them home. This was the exciting moment, the moment we waited for when we would learn how much our birds loved us. It was also the moment when we learned how much the pigeons loved each other when the males proved how handsome they were and the females proved how pretty. Some would fly straight home but others would fall in love with each other and follow their mates to a new home.

I was good at this sport because I had a special bond with my pigeons due to the fact that I had raised them from a very young age, so most of the time I came out a winner. Sometimes my birds would bring home new additions. If I flew twenty, sometimes when they came back there would be two or three new faces. It was my job then to make sure that they too stayed with me and did not leave.

August evenings in Peshawar were hot and humid. We had a small house so we used to sleep on the rooftop where the air was always cooler. I remember sleeping under the stars, thinking only about my pigeons and the new friends they brought home. As I fell asleep, I would think about how I would keep them, and how they would never want to leave.

But over time my parents became concerned that I was spending too much time with my pigeons, and my mother became frustrated with the droppings around the house, so they decided to give my birds away.

There was one special pigeon with reddish-brown wings and a whitish body. She was my favorite. I don't know how, but when you are a child you have a gift for recognizing special qualities, even in pigeons. I presume birds have that sense as well. My favorite was given to family friends who lived about 200 miles away, with instructions to make sure she would not come back to me. I was devastated for weeks.

Our friends trimmed her wings to make sure she could not fly far, in the hope that she would forget me and the house where we lived. Slowly, as we all know, memories fade away and I got used to my life without my pet pigeons. Then, one evening, when I was sitting on the roof watching the kites and pigeons flying overhead, I heard the rustle of wings behind me. I jumped up in amazement and could not believe my eyes to see my favorite pigeon landing on the roof. I was amazed that she had flown all this way — two hundred miles— to come back. She probably stopped in a few places to spend the night, perhaps forgoing food and water. When I think back, I do not know what desires or feelings drove her to make this journey. But somehow I knew that she would return. It is still amazing to me, how a small bird made me so happy. That feeling still lives in my soul after all these years.

Even after my pigeons were gone, the rooftops of Peshawar continued to be magical, strange, and sometimes violent places. From up high, you would see all kinds of things in the sky — pigeons, kites, bullets — all flying around at the same time. Most household owned guns and people would shoot up in the air for entertainment or to celebrate important events like birthdays and weddings. I often saw the red tracers of Kalashnikov rifles overhead. If you were in the wrong place at the wrong time, you could easily be hit by a stray bullet (the most common injury in Peshawar). I tried to be so careful up there.

Nevertheless, the rooftops were important and popular sites, especially for kite-flying battles. These battles were a favorite pastime and everyone including children, adults, and sometimes whole families would be involved. In the evening, people would gather on the rooftops to compete or just to witness the action high up in the sky. My father was against this practice and regarded it as a complete waste of time. So I was the only one in my family who would quietly go to the rooftop to participate in this exciting sport. The object of the game was to pull your kite into a dive and use your string to attack the string of another kite. When the two strings rubbed against each other, depending on the force and speed of the attack, and on which kite attacked from the top, one of the strings would break and a kite would fly away, never to be reclaimed by its owner since there were always young kids waiting in the streets and on the rooftops, ready to scurry away with the loser.

I recall one August afternoon when I was twelve years old. It was warm and breezy and the sun was shining. I stood on the roof of my house and watched the rainbows dancing in the sky, beautiful wings of yellow, orange, purple, blue. High and low, big and small, in all shapes.

My own kite was beautiful, red and white and floating with dozens of others around it. As the evening progressed, and as the battles raged, there were fewer and fewer left behind.

A large green kite inched closer to my own and I knew the game was on. I had no idea who was flying the kite. All I could see was that it was getting closer and closer and I knew what was coming.

I knew that my string was strong and razor-sharp. We would spend hours preparing different coatings of Manja to make them sharp enough to knife through their opponents. Manja usually contained glue with finally powered glass for sharpness. Everyone had their own secret recipes to make the string strong and sharp. I recently covered mine with a coating of shiny liquid.

The two strings hugged each other. I felt the friction when I pulled. Then I loosened my grip to move my kite away. Then I tightened again and pulled back to make it rise. And suddenly I had the top position. I pulled and loosened in quick succession as the strings hugged, kissed, sawed, pushed, and snapped. I felt the other kite breaking loose and watched it drift away.

For a brief moment, I enjoyed my victory. Then I was challenged again, twice, losing my third match of the evening. But I stayed on the roof for the rest of the evening to witness the last battles as darkness approached Peshawar.

Chapter 8
Drum Beat At Night

It would be unthinkable for anyone in the West to play loud drums in the streets before sunrise. I am sure the cops would be called and probably the person or people would be arrested and taken for psychological analysis. But, as a child, I remember waking up in the middle of the night to the sounds of drum beats. The man beating the drum was about five feet tall and he walked with a limp, probably due to polio. He usually arrived on our street around 3 a.m., and in addition to the beat of his drum he would shout, "Wake up! Wake up!".

Some may wonder why someone was allowed to make such noise at such an unholy hour, but in fact, the purpose of this noise was entirely for Holy reasons. His job was to wake people up in preparation for the fast during the month of Ramadan. He was reminding people to prepare the Sahari, which is the food eaten before sunrise when the fast begins. There were others who would also come wandering through the streets of Peshawar in the middle of the night. Some would knock on people's doors with loud bangs, others would play musical instruments or ring a bell. The idea was that by waking people up during this holy month they would earn favor with God. The ritual of fasting requires no eating or drinking between sunrise and sunset. The fast starts by eating a full meal, Sahari, before sunrise and it ends with a meal after sunset called Iftar.

Imagine waking up in the middle of the night to eat? It might make some people cranky, but I remember being very excited about it. Yawning, with eyes still half-closed, and with the excitement of a change in the routine, I looked forward to hearing this man chant to the beat of his drum. In my family, we gathered to eat a special breakfast of naan and paratha with a special dessert called halwa. The month of Ramadan provided a change in the routine for everyone. People fast in the hope of wiping away their sins and waiting for the big celebration of Eid which is also called the Festival of Breaking the Fast. Because of the hardships inherent in fasting every day for a month, some people used the fast as an excuse to not work as hard.

During Ramadan, the food shops and restaurants would be closed all day, but in the evening the bazaars were full of people buying all kinds of treats for Iftar. The Iftar was a big occasion with all kinds of food. Whole families would sit around and eat together. I remember one evening, about an hour before Iftar, two of my friends and I were shopping for some samosa and pakora. The whole place was bustling with people who were buying all kinds of treats, and everyone was hungry. My friend's car got a slight scratch from the motorbike of a middle-aged man who was riding with his young daughter. My short-tempered friend got out of his car and when he saw the scratch on his car (remember there was no concept of car insurance in the country), he got very angry and slapped the man across his face. This, of course, resulted in a huge altercation. People immediately gathered to break the quarrel. It was a severe insult to slap someone in public, especially an older person who was with his child. Suddenly, one of the fruit-sellers from the bazaar pulled a knife from his pocket and jumped into the fray. I am not sure if he knew the gentleman or if he was just defending him because of a common code of respect. Realizing that this was becoming a very bad situation, I intervened with a very convincing apology on behalf of my friend. The fruit-seller put his knife back in his pocket and my friend and the motorbike driver came to an understanding about the scratch on the car. Unfortunately, because people were so hungry, weary, and yes, cranky from fasting all day, these types of altercations were all too common in the late hours of Ramadan evenings before the break of the fast.

As the month of Ramadan neared its end, people would begin to prepare for Eid. After a full month of fasting, everybody was very excited about the Eid celebration. I was always very happy about the new clothes and shoes that were the usual gift for the occasion. I was also excited to get Eidi which is a cash award given to children by their elders. There were huge celebrations with lots of food, as well as visits from friends and family. And finally, on the day of Eid, we also saw the men who were involved in the middle of the night wake-up rituals for one last time. They visited all the houses expecting to be paid for their impeccable wake-up services.

The second Eid, which comes after about two months of the first one, celebrates the great act of obedience to Allah by the Prophet Ibrahim in his willingness to sacrifice his son Ismael. Allah accepted his sacrifice and replaced the Prophet Ismael with a lamb. Every year during the festival, Muslims around the world sacrifice an animal such as a goat, sheep, cow, or camel. The meat is divided into different parts and distributed among the poor, friends, and family. A few days before the celebration my family would go to the market to buy a lamb. I was always very excited about this. As a child, I loved all kinds of animals. The lamb would be in our house for about a week. I took care of it, inevitably, I became very attached to it. Knowing that the lamb would be sacrificed on the day of Eid made me sad and I would lie in my bed awake at night thinking about it. This celebration of Eid was a mixed bag for me. I was excited about the feast, but I always found it very hard to say goodbye to the lamb.

Chapter 9
I Do Not Like Closures

When I was about 12 years old, I remember opening the door of my childhood home to a middle-aged man dressed in a suit and tie. Seeing him dressed like that, I immediately knew that he was an important person. As a child growing up in that part of the world, a suit and tie was a symbol of power and importance. He asked me if my father was at home. I brought him into our very small sitting room. This was the room that we children were not allowed to go into as it was reserved for guests. When my father saw who his visitor was he became very happy because he immediately understood the reason for the visit. The man brought the news of my father being awarded the Presidential Medal for Education. My father was, understandably, very proud of this achievement. For an ordinary principal of a public school in Peshawar to receive one of the highest honors of our country was unheard of. He was given this award because of his extraordinary hard work and dedication to his students. His was a public school with very limited resources, but his students were securing top positions in the province on a consistent basis.

Where I grew up there was huge financial and societal inequality. Most people, including my family, were poor but there were also very wealthy families.

Those families had lots of property and wealth. They lived in big mansions and had nothing in common with ordinary people. Most of them were landowners or businessmen. The British encouraged this type of society. By keeping the very few wealthy families close to themselves, they were able to keep the country in their control. Massive amounts of land were awarded to these families by the British government in return for their loyalty. These families typically educated their children abroad in very expensive private schools.

The poor, on the other hand, had very little chance of succeeding in life. For the people born in a lower class, it was nearly impossible to move upward. No matter how hard people worked or tried, the doors of progress were shut to them, and ultimately they would realize that people were not supposed to change their class. The only real way out of this was to get a good education. A good education was the key to improving one's chance of a better life. The problem was that the public schools were in a very bad state.

My father, through hard work and determination, was able to dramatically change the lives of the children he taught by providing them with an excellent education. Most of his students became very valuable members of society. Many became doctors, engineers, lawyers, and bankers who, in turn, did good things for their families and for society in general. When I think of his contribution to the society of Peshawar, my respect for my father increases tremendously. I know from my experience and my understanding of the world that most of these kids would not have had any future if they had not come in contact with my father.

As humans, we tend to not appreciate things until they are gone. We take loved ones for granted and think that they'll be around forever. Only when they are gone do we realize how important they were in our lives and how we miss their presence. Men, in general, have a special bond with their fathers. I always shared my successes with my father in a way that I never shared with anyone else. I guess I wanted to make him proud. I still don't know why I wanted to do this. He never expected anything extraordinary from me, but I always felt the need to please him.

Now that I have seen and experienced a few things in life, I can honestly say that his contribution to the improvement of society was huge. In comparison to him, I do not think that I can even come close to his achievements. My father was a very liberal man with no strict religious affiliation. He married my mother at a young age, and they remained married until he died.

The last time I saw my father he looked thin and weak, but he was still mentally sharp. We enjoyed being in each other's company.

After about two weeks of my visit, he had fallen and had a concussion. I was not able to attend his funeral, but according to my family, it was very well attended. That alone was a testament to his contributions to his community. It showed respect and appreciation from all the people he helped. Many newspapers wrote special articles about his achievements.

I was sorry to miss his funeral, but there was also part of me that did not want to see his dead body. I wanted to remember him as I saw him on my last visit. I have never felt comfortable with death. I want to ignore death. I do not like the idea of losing a loved one and I don't want to accept it. As a child, I was fearful of death. After a neighbor or other person from the community died, I would often have sleepless nights wondering and worrying about them. I avoided discussing anything about them, and that is exactly how I dealt with things when my father died. I celebrated his life without thinking about his dead body.

I do not like closures. I want these chapters in my life to remain open. The closure will come when I die. Until then, I continue to think that my loved ones are still around me. I have my father's photograph in my house and every day I say hello to him. He is not physically present, but I feel his presence all the time.

Chapter 10
Early (so-called) Education

As a child, I dreaded going to school, so much that I often pretended to be ill with a stomach ache or an earache — anything to keep me from going back to a place I thought of as a prison. There were no desks or benches. The teacher sat in a chair and all the kids (thirty or forty to a class) would sit on the floor facing him. There wasn't a cafeteria or library. Each of us was given a wooden board with a handle on one side. On that board, we practiced our lessons. We would write them and then wipe them off repeating this process over and over while the teachers threatened us with their canes. Every child was afraid of the beatings from teachers, which happened quite frequently. The beatings left marks on our bodies, but parents accepted and even appreciated these punishments as a sign that our teachers were doing their jobs by making an effort to teach unruly children. When I think back, I sometimes wonder what kind of traumas and scars — both literal and figurative — were imprinted on us by our teachers. The poorest children often had no place for comfort, neither in school nor at home. I know that teachers had good intentions but did not know any better.

Somehow I survived and managed to enroll in the high school where my father was the principal. I continued to be unhappy there. My father, who believed in a good education, knew of my desire to change schools. He looked for alternatives and found a boarding school about 40 miles from our home. It was one of the best schools in that part of the world providing many opportunities to its students including sports and other extracurricular activities. This school had a lot more to offer than the high school where my father taught. I am still not sure how he could afford the tuition on his salary, but I remember that he started to work very hard and he also started to tutor children at our house for extra money.

My boarding school was a lot better than many other schools around Peshawar but in no way could it compare to schools in the West. Now that I have seen the elite schools in the United States and in the United Kingdom, I realize just how different my schooling was. The comparison is mind-boggling. The access that students in elite schools in the West have to sports such as horseback riding, water polo, and archery, along with the availability of modern computers and cafeterias with all types of food is immense. And don't even get me started on the libraries with all the beautiful books, as well as the music, dance, and gymnastics classes, debating societies, and school magazines. It is hard for me to imagine any under-developed nations ever getting close to this type of education.

Of course, at the time, I didn't know anything about schools in other parts of the world. All I knew was that I was homesick. I cried every night for months after I left home. I missed my mother terribly. But there was always a new adventure too. To a young boy, even the trip on the bus seemed exciting.

On the way to my new school, the bus passed through the mountains in the tribal areas and stopped at a market for a short break. The location of this marketplace was the transitional area between the semi-autonomous tribal lands and Pakistan's North-West Frontier Province. It was a harsh territory along the Afghanistan border that had been drawn-up during colonial times by British diplomat Sir Henry Mortimer Durand as a means to divide and weaken the eleven major Pashtun tribes and turn Afghanistan into a buffer zone between the British and Russian empires. The Durand Line has never been recognized by Afghanistan so the boundary is fluid. There is no border security there, so, in effect, there is no border.

I liked getting off the bus and wandering through the different markets. Some vendors sold electronics or vegetables, while others sold opium and hashish, while others still sold guns. In these shops, anyone could buy handguns, shotguns, or even Kalashnikovs. I watched the customers testing their weapons at the roadside by firing shots in the air. At the time, I thought it was fun to watch this activity, but I would learn later what a very dangerous thing this is.

After settling in at school, I returned home for two nights every three weeks. I barely saw my father during these visits, but I clung to my mother, especially at the beginning. I was always ready to quit, but she kept encouraging me to continue my education in that school. She would tell me how much better my life would be if I got back on the bus and left my family in Peshawar. She was right, and soon I was thriving, and maybe even eager to leave home to go back to school.

I started to succeed in academics and in sports, but there were also challenges. I was from a more modest background than my classmates and I was a son of the partition. The students at this boarding school came from wealthy families — the sons of businesspeople and bureaucrats. In such a place, money and power were just as important as merit or achievement, and sometimes even more so. The wealthiest and most influential always found ways to help their children succeed or get ahead. Before the summer break following tenth grade, in front of all my classmates, I was told by our headteacher that I would be the proctor the following year. To be a proctor was a source of great pride and I was looking forward to returning to school. However, to my shock and to that of my classmates, I learned that another boy had been given the honor. That boy was the least deserving of my classmates, but we were given no explanation as to why I had been overlooked. However, about six months later, I learned that the boy's father was a wealthy man and had given the teacher's son a job in his company.

I continued to work hard and finished at the top of my class and was admitted to medical school. There were mainly two paths for most of the students after the intermediate examination, either to become an engineer or to pursue the study of medicine. Being a doctor was a dream for all the poor and lower-middle-class people in that country. My father's desire was to have one of his children become a doctor. In my family, I was the one getting good grades in school, so this was the path chosen for me.

Chapter 11
Ghost War

Sometimes friends appear in one's life randomly, as if from nowhere. Only a select few leave lifelong, lasting impressions. Their presence is felt as if they have become a part of your existence and you cannot separate them from your being. As I grew older and slowly started to detach myself from my home and family, memories of my youth would pop up from time to time. During these memories, there was one particularly special person who I thought of frequently.

Rahim was a boy I met when I was about eight or nine years old. In the evening, at dinner time, I would see him wandering the street with a small bucket in his hand. At first, I did not know who he was, where he lived, or what he was doing, but I began to notice him more and more. During our dinner, he would stand in the street, chanting and hitting the bucket with a small stick in order to attract our attention. Eventually, I found out that his parents had passed away and he now lived in the nearby mosque. Rahim was an orphan and a Talib. The Talibs were young boys living in nearby mosques under the care of the imam. In a sense, they are students (which is what the word "Talib" means), but they do not attend the usual schools. Instead, they are educated by their imams who teach them to memorize and recite the Quran. I have seen these boys in groups of about fifteen or twenty, sitting on the floor of the local mosque, reciting verses very loudly in Arabic. Most memorize the entire Quran this way. This is their education, handed down from the imam, who was probably also Talib and received his own education in this way.

In the evening, the Talib would wander around the neighborhood chanting, and looking for food for themselves as well as for their caretakers. That was the only way for them to feed themselves. Rahim came to our street regularly. I always looked out for him and made sure that his bucket was full. This interaction eventually became a routine. He didn't say much but he always gave me a look of gratitude, which as a child, I knew very well.

This went on for a few years. I would see him quite often and, gradually, we started to talk. He would tell me about his life in the mosque, and he would ask me about my schooling. Even as a child, I could feel the purity and innocence of his soul. We did not spend too much time together, but there was a silent bond between us, and in time a more profound friendship started to take hold.

He continued to live his simple and straightforward life, and I moved on to boarding school. I did not see him for long stretches of time, but whenever I came home, I would visit him at the mosque. He would tell me about his accomplishments, how he was teaching other young Talibs to read and memorize the Quran. At that time, this was the sole purpose of his life. Then, as I finished boarding school and started medical school, I went to visit him and I was told that he had gone to Afghanistan to fight with the Taliban against the Soviet Union.

When I finally did see him again a few months later, he looked well and seemed happy. He told me all about his battles against the Soviets. He was totally committed to going back to Afghanistan; back to the battle. He told me how proud he was to be fighting against the invaders who had taken over our country. He explained how, in one particular battle, a few Afghani fighters equipped with only a minimum of equipment had been able to defeat the strong Soviet army who were equipped with powerful tanks, helicopters, and planes. I could see the resolve in his face and I wondered how many young people had felt this way throughout the centuries — fighting for something they truly believed in.

Rahim tried to persuade me to go with him, but I did not have the same desire or conviction. Unfortunately, that was my last meeting with him. A few months later I learned that Rahim had died while fighting in Afghanistan. I was told that he fought bravely with his friends on the front lines.

I listened to this news and reflected on how sad it was that a young and beautiful soul had passed away. I was thinking of how many young people over the centuries have fought with the same purposefulness defending their land and culture from invaders like Alexander the Great, the Persians, the Aryans, the Mongols, the Mughals, and the British. I also wondered and worried about how long these types of conflicts will continue. We were currently battling the Soviets. Who would be next? The Americans? The

Europeans? Will the fighting ever end? Did Rahim die in vain?

I wondered how Rahim's life might have been different if he had not been orphaned, and then, because of that tragedy, been indoctrinated by the imams. If he had been given the opportunity to study history, culture, science, and math, as I had been, would he still have been as eager to lose his life for the Taliban? I wondered if it was better for him that he died a hero at a young age or would it have been better if he had lived a long life of wandering and acquiring knowledge and experience?

As I thought about my future, I began to wonder what the purpose of my life was. Rahim seemed to have a strong purpose, what was mine? Every life eventually comes to an end. Does it make a difference when life ends? What ending would I like people to conclude about my life? What purpose would I fulfill that would make me feel proud? Is a life without purpose a life worth mentioning? Is it better to die young knowing you have fulfilled your purpose or is it better to live a long life without any real conviction or purpose? I don't think I'll ever know the answer to these questions.

Chapter 12
My First Awakening

A few months after I learned of Rahim's death, I found myself in a place where all of my senses were on full alert. I was looking at a dissection table, smelling a pungent odor, and listening to the sounds of saws and scalpels. On the table was a cadaver — a dead body — that had been preserved with formaldehyde, hence the strong smells, sounds, and views I was experiencing.

I, and my fellow medical students, were spread out around the body. A few students were near the head and were using a saw to cut open his skull to get a closer look at his brain. Others were working with scalpels on his abdomen to access his organs, while even more students were near the lower part of the table, dissecting his legs and feet. We were all very busy examining the physical structures of the body. None of us knew how long he had been dead or even how he died. Nobody seemed to show any concern about his past life or if he had left any family behind. We were all there to learn anatomy from this poor soul who was stretched out in front of us. The scene reminded me of vultures attacking the body of an animal who died in a forest or desert. All were taking a piece of its flesh for their own taste and needs.

As I examined the fascinating craftsmanship of this human sculpture I was mystified by the beauty of the human body. I was thinking of the delicate connections of the nerves to the different parts of the body and was fascinated to see that the arteries and the nerves looked like the branches of a tree, supplying nutrition and sensations to the various body parts. The structure of the organs — the heart, the lungs, and the mighty brain —and the mastery of the smaller joints, which can move in many ways, had me mesmerized. I was also thinking about how hard the heart and lungs have to work to keep a continuous supply of fresh blood and oxygen to the body. Keep in mind that while all of these other things are working, the human ear works hard to differentiate all sounds while the eyes get to see all the beauty around us.

But as we were working on this particular body, I was suddenly hit with the reality of death. At a young age, it is difficult to grasp the concept of death because we all feel immortal when we are young. The thought of being mortal never crosses the youthful soul. However, anyone who has ever started medical school has to face the issue of mortality head-on. For many medical students, the dissection hall is where they have their first encounter with death.

That dead body in the dissection hall seemed to stare at me right in the eye. In human relationships, when you look deeply into someone's eyes, you seem to have a better connection with that person. There is a certain mysterious power in deep eye contact. It seems that by staring into someone's eyes you are looking into their soul; you create a special connection with them. For obvious reasons, there was none of that here. This body's eyes were cold and his soul was missing.

Most of the students that day didn't think about it too much and started to open the cavities, the joints, and the organs to get a closer picture of the workings of this beautiful and fascinating machine. But my mind was wondering about things that I was not supposed to be thinking of at that time. I was not sure who this person was and why he was lying on this table. I presumed that he was either a kind soul who volunteered his body for this final assault in order to benefit the human race, or he was one of those unfortunate people who had no choice in the matter. Life might have given him a miserable deal, and now the last insult was to have his body destroyed in this fashion.

I wondered if his soul had left him or if there was still some part of it lingering there to know what was happening to him. I thought about how the soul could be so selfish. How could it leave this body which had been its partner for so many decades? I questioned if it was the end or if there was still some presence of him in this universe. As the other students were talking about the anatomy of his veins and his muscles, I thought about what was there before, what made all these beautiful parts work together in harmony? What had changed that made this brilliant work of art so helpless, so rotten? From time to time during my daydreams about the cadaver, I would be awoken from my deep thoughts by the comments of fellow students who got excited when their scalpel uncovered something important like a hidden nerve or a vessel. At that moment I would admire the anatomy and then drift again into my deeper state of restlessness, confusion, and sadness.

I wanted to know more about the psyche of the human body as well as the physical aspects. How did his body end up here on this table? What was the purpose of his life and was it fulfilled? Did he leave any family behind? Was he loved by someone?

As I was learning to be a doctor, the destruction of his body was my path to resurrection. I did not want to waste more time thinking. I finally got my head in the game and joined the others who had already decided to proceed without much thought to these questions.

Chapter 13
My Friend's Dilemma

As I was nearing the end of my medical school training in Peshawar, my parents reminded me from time to time that I was getting older and they wanted to know if I was ready to settle down. They would tell me about certain girls that they thought were suitable for me to marry. But I wasn't ready for that. My friend, Kamran however, was on a direct path to an arranged marriage. Kamran was one of those people who come into one's life who, just by their mere presence, makes others happy.

Kamran was one of my best friends. He was over six feet tall, very lean with a beard and mustache. Of all my friends, I enjoyed his company the most. He brought life to any party and was always happy and full of energy. Everyone wanted to be in his company.

Our discussions were interesting. We had great chemistry, and we were always laughing together. In school, he and I would sit in the back of the class; he would sing, and I would drum the desk with my hands. We fed each other through our mutual energy and creativity. But sometimes in life, the more you get to know someone, the more they can surprise you. Kamran surprised me in many ways. He presented himself as a calm, happy, and cheerful person, but there was a deeper and more serious side to his personality. He hid that part of himself from everyone except his closest friends. He worked hard to keep people at bay and allowed only a few people to get close to him. He was restless. It took me years to fully understand him.

Kamran was very smart and observant, but he was also very conflicted. Like many people in that part of the country, Kamran was brought up in a strict, religious home. Because of that upbringing, he had a battle raging deep inside him about the rights and wrongs of daily living. As I mentioned before, he chose to fight against the Russians in Afghanistan.

During our teenage years, he would often be seen smoking, having fun, and cracking jokes at parties. Then, he would suddenly start to avoid these gatherings and instead would spend most of his time going to the mosque and talking with the mullahs and other religious scholars. Once in a while, we would hear that Kamran had gone away on a trip to preach Islam in other cities. After a few months, he would reappear as if nothing happened and he would start partying again. We all knew that he seemed to lead two different lives, but none of us cared; we were all just happy to see him.

Looking back now, I can totally relate to Kamran. As children, we were all brought up with fear, conflict, contradictions, and constant threats. Economics, poverty, lack of education, and poor health care lead to some of our fears but religion was, by far, the main focus of our fear.

I remember lying awake in bed worrying about the bad things that happened to children who did not obey religious teachings. The horrors of hell and burning alive in the fire were enough to keep any child awake at night. I know that parents had the best of intentions and wanted their children to be morally good but did not have the right approach. Kamran's family was particularly religious, however, he also liked to have fun, so as a result, he battled a lot of inner demons regarding what is sin and what is goodness. He was smart and had a vast imagination, so he was more troubled by these thoughts than the rest of us.

We were all very young, and it was a natural desire to seek interactions with girls, but we never had an opportunity to do so. Kamran, however, was not troubled by thoughts and desires about girls. According to his religious beliefs, it was considered a major sin to have any close social interaction with the opposite sex before marriage. He never had any close contact with a girl before he got married, as this would have gone against his Muslim religion.

While the rest of us were all still just dreaming about girls, Kamran's parents decided it was time for him to settle down and get married. He was the first one among all of my friends to get married, and he married entirely according to the customs and traditions of our culture. And even though he was entering into an arranged marriage, he was very excited about it. He saw it as a duty to his religion; love and passion did not factor into it.

Chapter 14
Arranged Marriage

It happened to be that my friend, Kamran's great aunt, who was about seventy years old was attending a wedding in Peshawar. She came across this young lady who was about twenty years of age. It is common back home for these older ladies, as a pastime, to be nosy and inquisitive, looking for gossip and something to do. She inquired about this young lady, who in her opinion was attractive, and after finding out that she was still single, she thought of her nephew, Kamran, who was of the right age to get married. She thought this match would be a good one and that's how it all started.

In the East, marriage is not just between two people; it bonds entire families together. When choosing a spouse not only the religion but the clan has to be the same as well. Parents will seek out a potential spouse for their child from a family with the same socio-economic circumstance as their own. They think that if one person is from a wealthy background and the other is from a more modest background it will not make a good match. They believe that the bride and groom might not adjust well to the habits of the other if their socioeconomic backgrounds are too different. So having the same religion, race, color, family clan, and socioeconomic status will be more likely to make the bond more lasting. With these similarities, it will be harder to break the family's ties that keep the two together. In simpler terms, an arranged marriage is not just between the bride and groom, but between two entire families.

The process starts when one family tells another family about a young woman who is at the right age to get married. The elders of both families will have a discussion among themselves. The groom's family, after learning about the young woman, will start to think about whether or not she is the right match for their son. At this stage probably neither the prospective bride or groom will have any idea that these discussions are happening. It's either the young woman's parents or grandparents, her uncles or aunts, or even some friends who will be involved in this step of the process. The bride is usually the last to know.

In shia culture, usually if the groom's parents want to pursue this potential arrangement further, they discuss it with a religious scholar (a person similar to a priest in the West). The scholar would then be given the task of finding out if this match is suitable. This is done by making religious inquiries as well as asking God for answers. It's all done in a very particular manner. The religious scholar recites some verses from the Quran, and after some prayers, he randomly opens the Quran. The interpretation of the open page is supposed to be God's will or desire for the match. If in the scholar's opinion, the description is good, this would indicate a good match. This would then be a signal for the boy's family to go and ask for the girl's hand from her parents.

The asking for the girl's hand is a formal ceremony of "engagement" in which the boy's parents and some of their relatives go to the girl's house with some sweets and other gifts to formally ask for their daughter to be married to their son. The girl's parents listen and then promise them a reply after they have considered the offer. They would then make some inquiries about the boy and his family. They would also go to their religious scholar and ask for the same type of religious inquiry that the boy's family had requested. If the interpretation is reasonable, they would then contact the boy's parents and accept the proposal. If the interpretation of the Quran's verse is not good, then they would respectfully decline the offer.

Kamran was very excited about his upcoming wedding. Although he had never been in love nor had he any idea of what love was, he could not wait for his wedding. He was not allowed to meet his intended wife before the ceremony. In fact, he had never even seen her. If he had been lucky enough to meet her, she would have been clad in a chador or a shawl. Kamran tried often to visualize her face and her features. He asked his sister to describe the girl and to tell him about her looks and her appearance. Everything was left to his imagination. I assume that if he had been in love before or had any encounters with women in the past, he might have known what to expect or how to react.

The whole concept of an arranged marriage is fascinating. I tried to imagine what Kamran's wedding night would be like. He was going to be in the company of a complete stranger; a person he had not only never seen before, but he had never even spoken to her. The same would be true for his wife. How do you form an intimacy that marriages require if you have never even spoken to your spouse? Imagine starting your married life in such a way? To this day, I still don't know how to get a real insight into the mind of the bride and groom when they face each other for the first time in an arranged marriage. What thoughts, what emotions, what hopes, dreams, fears, and uncertainties go through their minds? I imagine it is even more impossible for Westerners to imagine that interaction. If I had not lived in both the East and the West it would have been impossible for me to explain this drastic difference between the two cultures.

I, myself, came very close to an arranged marriage. In my case, I agreed to visit and meet the girl who my parents had decided I should marry. Both of my parents, my older sister, and I visited their family one evening. We brought sweets and fruit with us. The girl's family greeted us with great respect and anticipation. We all sat in one big room. My prospective bride sat in a corner of the room. She was very shy. The whole evening was very awkward for me. I assume it was at least equally uncomfortable for her. We were able to see each other, but we did not speak. Our parents talked to each other, and I had to answer some questions from her parents. I had no desire to pursue this arrangement any further and, fortunately, the Shia priest, who her parents asked to interpret the reading from the Quran, agreed that it would not be a good match.

In Eastern cultures, marriage celebrations usually last for over two weeks. Kamran's wedding was no exception. He got married and everyone present hoped that the union would last forever. Most arranged marriages do last a lifetime, but the question remains — what is this marriage? What is happiness in this type of relationship? Is it love?

Chapter 15
Food For Thought

I was awoken from my deep thoughts about the food that we were all looking forward to having that night when someone sitting beside me asked if I was a guest of the bride or the groom. This was an interesting question as I did not know either the bride or the groom. I didn't even know whose house or wedding I was attending. My table mate seemed to only want to make small talk so I told him that I was a friend of the bride's relatives. However, the story of how and why I was really there was far more mischievous.

But first, I will tell you a bit about Pakistani weddings. Pakistani weddings are large events, sometimes with hundreds of guests attending. Adults, children, friends, family, friends of family, neighbors, co-workers, and so many others might all be invited. The larger the wedding the better it is in regard to the family image and the showing off of their social status.

It is not unusual for a wedding celebration to last for a week or more with many different ceremonies. In one of the first celebrations, friends, and families gather to play and listen to songs and music. Girls sing along with small drums called dholak. The next ceremony is the Mehndi. This is one of the most important events. The bride wears colorful clothes and her arms, hands, and feet are decorated in beautiful, flowery patterns with mehndi — a paste made from dried leaves called henna. The Mehndi is brought by the groom's family and the night is celebrated with more songs, dances, and food.

About two or three days before the wedding, the bride is sequestered in anticipation of the wedding in a ceremony called Mayun. The bride usually wears a colorful dress. During this ceremony, a special yellow liquid made from turmeric, perfumes, and oils is applied to the bride's skin brought by the family of the groom. This is supposed to make the bride's skin soft and shiny. This ceremony is also accompanied by music, dancing, and fantastic food. After this ceremony, the bride is forbidden to do any household tasks. She is supposed to rest and relax while listening to music and enjoying the company of her friends and family during her final days at her parent's house. The Mayun is also another excuse to get together with lots of music, dancing, talking, and food.

The formal and most important ceremony of Nikah happens next. This is where the legal documents are signed by the bride and the groom in the company of their witnesses. The document's name is Nikka Namma which is a detailed contract explaining all the terms and conditions agreed to by the two families.

The Rukhsati is the departure of the bride from her parent's house to the groom's house. It can be a sad and emotional event for the bride's parents and her family. The last and final event is the Walima. This is a lunch or dinner reception by the groom's family. Hundreds of people are invited to attend this event. There is usually a grand stage where the bride and groom sit. They are both dressed in beautifully decorated garments surrounded by friends and family. This event is the final stage of the wedding and the newly married couple can start their new life together.

There is, however, one other celebration that occurs between the Nikka Namma and the Rukhsati. This event is called the Barat and this is where my story continues. The Barat is when the groom's family, friends and many other invited guests travel in a big procession to the bride's house. Some processions involve traveling in a large procession of cars and some involve the groom arriving on a lavishly decorated horse accompanied by music and drums. The event is organized by the bride's family. Typically lots of exotic foods and desserts are served to the arriving guests. The bride's family takes it as an honor to entertain all the guests in the groom's party. They are determined to treat everyone nicely and show hospitality towards their guests.

I once attended a medical course in Karachi with two of my friends. We were there in November which just happens to be in the middle of "wedding season". The wedding season typically runs from October to March and during this time many weddings occur almost every evening. Karachi is the biggest city in Pakistan with a population of over ten million people. Weddings in certain wealthy parts of Karachi tend to be very large and extravagant. When I was there with two of my friends, we were staying in a hostel. We had a lot of free time but not much money. We also had a mutual friend who was studying in Karachi and knew the city very well. Fortunately, he also had a car. In the evenings we dressed up nicely in shirts and ties and drove around the wealthy neighborhoods. We could tell by the size of the house and the decorations that there was to be a big wedding that night. When we saw a Barat with lots of cars, we would simply join in the procession and then enter the bride's house with everyone else. We would enjoy the celebrations including a wonderful meal of pilau rice, chicken tikka, kebabs, lamb, and so many excellent desserts including kheer and halwa, my favorite. And it was at one of these Barat celebrations when I was asked by my table-mate if I was a friend of the bride or the groom.

We repeated this same routine night after night. We had great fun looking for the most extravagant and lavish weddings among the many that were happening in that city. Sometimes we would attend two weddings in one night to try the different food choices. Once we met some people who we had seen at one of the previous weddings. I'm not sure if they were in the same game as us. After all, we were the original wedding crashers.

Chapter 16
There Will Always Be Change

The next time I saw Kamran, he'd been married for a few weeks. He seemed very happy. He told me all about his new life and how he had fallen in love with his wife. I wondered how he could have fallen in love so quickly with a woman he hardly knew. I assumed that, perhaps, it was because he was young and inexperienced, not only with women but with the world as a whole. Remember, he'd never had any interaction with another woman before his wedding, nor had he ever traveled outside of our region.

Young people are impulsive, which is a beautiful thing. They don't think or care too much about the future. They live in the moment, but time and age can radically alter a person's love life. For example, if a couple meets and falls in love with each other at the age of 18, there is a good chance that in just a few years, both people will be very different and may no longer love each other. Everyone changes with time and age due to life's experiences. Their priorities change, their tastes change, and, ultimately, who they love can also change. In the West, it is easier to walk away from a marriage because, in the beginning, there are only two people involved. But in the East, from the very start of the relationship, entire extended families are involved. Couples in the East feel guilty for breaking the bond of marriage because it affects so many other people. They will try their best to make the marriage work. Some people might argue that one should not be living with someone just for other people's sake. This is true, but in Eastern cultures, there is a lot more involved. In my culture, you learn to love the person you married because you have no other comparisons. Even in the West where there is openness and freedom, most people fall in love with a person they meet early in life — perhaps in school/college or at work. But for people that have been able to travel and have had the opportunity to meet people outside of their region, they might have a chance of falling in love with people from faraway lands and/or cultures and with whom they might have a deeper, more lasting relationship.

My point is that people cannot love someone until they have met them, and it is harder to meet them if their exposure is limited. In the East, people fall in love (or what they understand as love) because of very limited exposure. The boy/man gets exposed to only one girl/woman, and vice versa. It's like knowing only one type of food. If you have not been exposed to other kinds of foods, you have no comparison. It becomes a habit, and you start to like it because you don't know what else is out there. But when you have tasted Italian, Chinese, Mexican, and all other types of food, your taste gets refined and you think about your food choices. Similarly, if you live in a cold and damp climate and have never traveled to other places, it's hard to know what it's like to live in a place where the sun shines every day, that the ocean water can be warm, that birds sing and soar about.

This is what exposure to other cultures and traveling can do for you. That's what meeting other people does for you. That's when you start to wonder what love is.

What some people consider to be love could simply be limited exposure with limited knowledge and limited experiences in life. As people mature and have more life experiences they may begin to question their past choices. Confusion about the decisions that were made in the past can set in. Under these circumstances and these types of questions some marriages/relationships might begin to fall apart.

By most measures — both the East and the West - Kamran's marriage was successful. He and his wife lived in a nice, stable home surrounded by their larger family. They had four children — two sons and two daughters — all of whom were educated. Kamran and his wife did things as a couple, however, they did those things without much thought as to whether or not either of them really enjoyed or were even interested in them. As a couple, they tried to avoid conflicts between themselves because they were more concerned with the illusion of happiness and keeping their extended families happy. It was a safe marriage that survived the test of time, but it lacked passion. There weren't any incidences of extreme joy and/or sorrow that is usually part of a long-term, successful relationship. It makes one wonder: Is marriage truly successful, no matter how long it is if there is no passion?

As time passed and Kamran's children grew-up, they started to break away from ancient traditions. In many ways they were being influenced by social media; they now had contact, inspirations, interactions, and, perhaps, interference from the rest of the world. As they became adults they wanted to try new things, and there was no way that Kamran would be able to stop them from venturing out. He wanted desperately to keep his kids within the boundaries of his culture and traditions, knowing that moving beyond these barriers might mean a major change for the whole family. However, none of his children wanted any compromises in their life. They wanted to try new things in order to find more pleasure and excitement in their lives. None of them had an arranged marriage.

None of us, not even Kamran, can predict how his kid's marriages will fare. Will they be like Western marriages in which there are extreme peaks of pleasure as well as deep valleys of sorrow? If so, because of these extremes, are they doomed to failure? And if they do fail, how might that impact Kamran's grandchildren? Will they have a stable home to live in or will they be shuttled from one household to another after their parents have split? Will they have any values to cling to? The only predictable thing in life is change. The change will always happen, even in Eastern cultures that are trying to avoid it at all costs.

Having traveled and been exposed to many cultures has changed my priorities. It has freed me from social constraints. The East is still trying to desperately hold on to old traditions, but the young people are moving on. They don't have time for old, rusty values and traditions. Everyone is in a hurry. The internet and social media have created a revolution of uncertainty, restlessness, and upheaval among the cultures which were once secluded. These cultures and societies have been awakened from their peaceful slumber. The changes which used to be limited to some countries or regions now spread like wildfire. The days of people clinging to their values and customs are coming to a quick end. Soon every person will be demanding liberty and freedom from the chains of past traditions and values that were keeping them in check. Unwritten morals, social customs, and traditions will soon give way to actual laws that everyone will need to abide by. People will start to behave in a certain way, not because they should or because it is the way their family has always behaved, but because they are afraid to break the laws that will soon replace moral obligations.

Chapter 17
My Friend With (no) Religion

When I was growing up, most of the people I knew spoke two or three languages. We did not learn the languages in school; we learned them on the streets of our multicultural city. The people of Peshawar were a mixture of many different ethnicities. We shared the same city, but the language, culture, food, traditions, and customs were all different. We learned other languages by playing with other kids and by communicating with shop owners and other ordinary citizens.

My friend Hamza was from Multan, a city in Southern Punjab. His native tongue was Saraiki, also called Multani. As mentioned earlier, he was the guy who saved the young girl in the bomb blast. My other friend Kamran spoke Pushto which was the language of the tribes settled close to the Afghan border. Peshawari, another language in our area, was similar to Punjabi spoken in the eastern part of Pakistan close to the Indian border. Urdu was the national language that was spoken and understood by all. Arabic, on the other hand, was a common language, and everyone was expected to know a bit of Arabic because it was the language of the Quran, the holy book of Islam. It was mostly a religious language used solely in the mosques and during prayer time.

Hamza was a handsome man and had a fair complexion with brown hair and light green eyes. He usually dressed in the western style clothes of shirt and trousers. According to Hamza, his ancestors were related to Alexander the Great who conquered Multan in 326 BCE. He had a good sense of style and always appeared very well put together. He was laid back, thoughtful in his conversations, and did not speak much but listened very carefully. He always appeared content, and he never seemed worried about anything. We all used to be anxious during our medical school exams, but Hamza never showed any signs of anxiety. He reminded me of Sufis or Darwish, the type of people who do not desire more from life but go with the flow and take every day as it comes.

Hamza was a true and trustworthy friend. There is one story in particular that epitomizes Hamza's true nature. When Hamza was in high school a classmate of his wanted to go to the neighboring girl's school to meet with a girl, he had a crush on. However, being in a Muslim country, boys and girls were kept strictly separated in all facets of life. For a boy to be caught in a girl's school was a very serious offense. But, being young and immature Hamza decided to accompany his friend, and sure enough, they got caught. Hamza's friend blamed the entire incident on Hamza. Hamza neither denied nor confirmed the accusation because he did not want his friend to get in trouble. As a result, Hamza was expelled from his prestigious school. But he was happy to take the expulsion rather than break the honor code of never betraying a friend. On another occasion, when someone stole a large sum of money from his room, he did not get angry or upset as most people would. Instead, he calmly said that the person who stole his money probably needed it more than he did.

There are two major factions in the religion of Islam — Shia, and Sunni — and they have a long history of conflict and rivalry. Hamza and I were Shia Muslims growing up in a predominantly Sunni Muslim country. This created a bit of a special bond between us. Among Muslim communities, Sunnis Muslims are a majority in Asia, Africa, most of the Arab World, and the United States. Shia Muslims make up most of the Muslim population in Iran, Iraq, and Bahrain. Minority communities are also found in Lebanon, Yemen, and Pakistan. Shias make up only about 10 to 15% of the entire Muslim world. Both Sunnis and Shias – drawing their faith and practice from the Quran and the life of the Prophet Muhammad – agree on most of the fundamentals of Islam. The differences are related more to historical events and issues of leadership.

The central difference emerged after the death of the Prophet Muhammad in AD 632. The issue was who would be the caliph — the "deputy of God" — after the Prophet. While the majority wanted Abu Bakr, one of the Prophet's closest companions, a minority opted for his son-in-law and cousin – Ali. Subsequently, those Muslims who favored Abu Bakr came to be called Sunni - "those who follow the Sunnah," the sayings and traditions of the Prophet Muhammad - and those who trusted in Ali came to be known as Shia - followers of "Shiat Ali," meaning "partisans of Ali". Abu Bakr became the first caliph, and Ali became the fourth caliph. The battle of

Karbala is the most significant event in the history of Shia Muslims. Ali's youngest son, Hussein was killed during that battle.

Hussein became a martyr. The day of the battle is commemorated every year on the Day of Ashura. Held on the tenth day of Muharram in the Islamic lunar calendar, scores of pilgrims visit Hussein's shrine in Karbala and many Shia communities participate in symbolic acts of flagellation and suffering.

Hamza always maintained that he did not have any religious biases but the sacrifice of Hussein, was an event that Hamza was very proud of. He made every effort during the first ten days of Muharram to remind everyone about the event. Coming from a well-to-do family, he inherited the Imambara (Shia mosque) that he proudly managed during Muharram. He was a boarding student at the Medical school in Peshawar and was not able to be there all the time. Occasionally, the Imambara would be damaged by the locals who did not like the Shia Muslims praying in that place. Hamza, as usual, would not have any bad feelings toward anyone and would simply ignore the foul play.

Although Hamza claimed to not be religious, he was actually quite spiritual and philosophical. While hanging around with the guys, if the discussion came around to theological subjects, Hamza would stay quiet. He would sit back, light a cigarette, (he was a chain smoker) take a few puffs, and listen, but he would not participate in the discussion. Most of our friends were Sunnis. As Shias, Hamza, and I would often be teased by our friends, it was all in good fun.

Unfortunately, even though my friends and I could overlook our religious differences, there were always tensions in different parts of Pakistan. The Imambaras would be damaged, and sometimes the attacks would result in deaths, but we, as friends, did not let those attacks come between us.

After one particular incident, I asked Hamza about his feelings toward the Sunnis, who had been responsible for so much harm and anguish to his Imambara. He lit a cigarette and took a deep puff before answering. He said that he could not understand why one type of religious celebration would anger other people and why so many people were concerned about what other people choose to celebrate or believe in. He wanted to celebrate everything with everyone to share in other people's joy, excitement, and happiness even though he did not share their religion. He was a champion of happiness, peace, and harmony. He participated in the celebration of Diwali by Hindus and used to be very happy during Christmas and Easter (Hindus and Christians, were two of the minorities living in Peshawar at the time). He was also aware of people who were well-traveled and educated but were still narrow-minded and were offended by other people's religious beliefs. He was a firm believer that people from different religions, factions, customs, and traditions can form a community and can share each other's happiness and live in peace and harmony. He thought that it's the responsibility of the educated class to understand and to teach the ignorant and small-minded people that living together in harmony is one of the greatest virtues of human beings. It was

Hamza's belief and it is also mine that when people of different backgrounds interact and get to know each other, they find a lot of common ground and become more tolerant of each other's differences.

Chapter 18
Unexpected Turn of Events

Heera Mandi, a red-light district located south of the Badshahi Mosque, is an area in the old city of Lahore. It is also called Diamond Market. The word Heera means diamond in Urdu and the word Mandi means market. The locals usually say that the name of Heera Mandi refers to the beauty of the girls in the market, but, in fact, the market is actually named after Heera Singh, who was the son of a minister of Ranjit Singh's court. Due to the history of royals and nobles of the Mughal empire coming to the area for entertainment and its location being close to the Lahore Fort, the neighborhood is sometimes also referred to as Shahi Mohalla, meaning "The Royal Neighborhood".

During fifteen and sixteenth centuries, the market was known for the city's concubine culture but later it became a center for mujra, a sensual South Asian dance performed by women and khusra (transgenders). Gradually overtime it became a hub for prostitution with the emergence of the brothel houses.

The brothel houses became popular and were frequently visited by the British soldiers for entertainment purposes during the British reign. During the daytime Heera Mandi is much like any other Pakistani bazaar with shops selling local footwear, clothes and restaurants serving local cuisine. At night, the brothels above the shops open. It is surprising to know that in such a strict Islamic country, this area is still flourishing and visited by many people every evening.

In the small houses above the shops, people walk in to see the dances being performed by the girls. These girls are mostly young and good-looking. They perform dances in the center of the room to different types of music while men sit on the floor around them on a colorfully carpeted floor. The dancers usually are dressed in tight shalwar kameez and pajamas, remain clothed throughout the performance, showing only their waist, part of the back, or bare arms. The erotic aspect of dancing between one woman and many men is mostly achieved through suggestions while they dance to Bollywood and Indian music. The dancers use fleeting eye contact, pointing, gesturing which make their targeted audiences "feel special". There is no physical contact between the girls and the patrons. The patrons shower the dancers with money, which generally results in more animated dancing. In some cases, the men would even garland the dancer with rupees. Many dancers depending on their beauty and dancing talents can make a lot of money in one night, thanks to the wealthy, and possibly drunken patrons. At the end of the evening, each girl's earnings are counted and split between the girls and the male protectors. In many cultures, these girls would be regarded as low class and the men would only go to them for entertainment purposes, not for a long-term relationship or commitment.

One evening six of us went to this market. We walked into one of the houses and asked to see the dance. We were directed to a room and after about ten minutes a girl named Rukhsana appeared from the side door and began dancing for us.

Rukhsana was a very pretty girl, in her early 20s, with long black hair and beautiful brown eyes. She was wearing a red dress embroidered with shiny decorations. Her hands had henna tattoos in a flowery pattern and on her wrists, she wore multiple colored bangles. She was a beautiful dancer and the evening was quite lovely. All of us who grew up in the most conservative parts of Pakistan were fascinated by this spectacle, and we were in awe of being in such close proximity to a beautiful young woman. We followed protocol and began to throw money at her as she was dancing. We tossed rupees on her every move as we were all young and were fascinated by this rare experience. This was the first time for most of us in such a place, and as we were all young and naive, we were all falling in love with this beautiful lady.

I noticed that Hamza, in particular, was very interested and continued to praise her every move. He gave her more money than the rest of us did. After about an hour of dancing, we were supposed to leave. As we all got up to go downstairs, Hamza suddenly turned and went to talk to Rukhsana. In less than one minute two men came after him and escorted him outside. His request to speak with her was utterly useless. Later that evening we went to a restaurant and I learned that Hamza had tossed all of his money to Rukhsana and he did not have any money left for his food. I was glad to lend him some.

At Hamza's insistence, we went to "visit" Rukhsana again two days later. He had an uncle living in Lahore, and he borrowed money from him. We knocked at the door of Rukhsana's house, but we were told that she was entertaining another party and was not available. Hamza was very disappointed and insisted we try again later that evening. We were successful in our second attempt to see Rukhsana dance that night. When she came into the room she gave us all a big smile. I am sure she has been giving that same smile to everyone who has ever come to watch her dance. We stayed for an hour during which time Hamza again gave her most of his money. Afterward, he tried to speak with Rukhsana again, but he was once again thwarted by the two bouncers.

The next day we left Lahore and went back to Peshawar. We all had a good time in Lahore but Hamza was somewhat quieter and seemed lost in his thoughts. After some digging, he told me that he had finally succeeded in talking to Rukhsana as he visited the house early next morning. Her story was very sad. She grew up in a small village in the region of Swat, which is the most beautiful part of Pakistan. Her parents were very poor and therefore could not take care of her properly. As she was a pretty girl, her parents were approached by some "business people" of Heera Mandi, and she was placed under their care. At the time that Hamza spoke to her, she had been living in the dance house for seven years and had been entertaining all kinds of people. She was very popular because of her beauty and dancing skills. She told him that she was the attention of many wealthy people who would regularly attend her dance sessions. She had no control over her income or her life for that matter. She was under the supervision of an old lady that she referred to as her mother. The old lady had two sons (the bouncers) who kept all the clients away from her as she was the only source of their income. She had nowhere to go and she was afraid of what might happen to her if she left the house. She had no contact with her biological parents. Knowing Hamza, I knew that on top of her beauty, the story must have had some influence on him. The way he talked about her, I got the feeling that he had fallen in love with her. Hamza was sad for her and her circumstances and it seemed like he was eager to take her out of that life.

Chapter 19
Love Is Complicated

Sometime later, as I was waiting for my visa to leave Pakistan, Hamza asked me to accompany him to visit Rukhsana in Lahore. While he was in the dance house I waited for him in a restaurant across the street. I ordered a cup of tea and wondered about the "whys" of love. Why do some people fall in love with a particular person? Young people are full of energy with few inhibitions or constraints. They tend to go with the flow and live in the moment. They fall in love very quickly as their impulsiveness overcomes reason or rationality. Hamza was definitely the "go with the flow" type. He was a very carefree person. I saw the twinkle in his eyes the very first time he met Rukhsana, and I knew that something about this girl touched him deeply. His love for her became even stronger when he learned her story. I believe that it was his desire to help her, combined with her beauty, that brought about his feelings of love for her. He was now a prisoner of his emotions and I knew that there was probably no escape for him. I was not sure he would be able to move on from this.

In contrast, when Kamran told me how quickly he had fallen in love with his new wife, I knew that in his case, it was his upbringing and religious teachings that played a key role in how quickly he fell in love.

Kamran was determined to fall in love with his wife because she had been — and would forever be — his only interaction with the opposite sex. His decision was made by his parents. He was not in control of the situation, but he was comfortable with this.

I was thinking about all these things when I saw some other men approaching the house where Rukhsana danced. I was certain that as soon as Hamza left Rukhsana, it would be their turn to be entertained by her. After about an hour, Hamza came out of the hall. He was happy and excited. He described how nice it was to be in Rukhsana's company. He told me she looked beautiful in her yellow dress and how he enjoyed the smell of her perfume. He also told me how happy she was when he gave her a beautiful (and I might mention expensive) necklace that he had bought for her. He was in love. However, as he was telling me all about Rukhsana, I saw the next set of men to go in to see her. I did not know how to tell Hamza that for Rukhsana, he was just another man in a long line of male admirers. For all, I know she may have also loved Hamza, but she was trapped; there was no way she could escape her bind.

Hamza was blinded by love, and he was in deep denial of the realities of the situation. No amount of explanation or evidence of the facts was going to sway him. Maybe he didn't want to know the real truth; we all want to hide away from life's harsh truths. Secretly I believed that Hamza may have thought he was in love, but in reality, it was just his good-hearted nature that didn't allow him to let other people suffer or live an unhappy life. He felt an enormous desire to rescue Rukhsana. He didn't care what others thought and therefore he was unconcerned about their opinions or how his actions might be perceived by others. He was so in love he thought that they could overcome any obstacle. And the obstacles were many.

Hamza's family was wealthy and well-respected, and they had a good standing in society. Social interaction was important in our part of the world and people were always interested in each other's business. The whole community was tightly knit, and people were keenly aware of other people's opinions. Everyone wanted to make others happy at the cost of their own happiness. So, it probably goes without saying that it was taboo for a man from a family such as Hamza's to be associated with a girl from Heera Mandi. Not only Hamza, but his entire family would suffer the social consequences of his relationship with her. He would be isolated from the community and his family would probably lose their reputation as decent, upstanding citizens. It would bring great shame to his whole family, and his parents would not be able to face anyone.

Regardless of this knowledge, in the coming months, Hamza continued to visit Rukhsana. Every time he visited, he would bring her expensive gifts. After about six months of this, he decided to propose to her. We both knew that Rukhsana was the only source of income for her adopted family. Knowing this, I knew they would probably never let her marry anyone, never mind Hamza. Hamza, however, felt confident because he knew that Rukhsana despised her life in Heera Mandi and that she loved him as much as he loved her. Sure enough, Rukhsana's family refused his proposal, even though Hamza offered them a large sum of money.

Chapter 20
Cycle Continues with No End

Hamza and Rukhsana's story did not end there. A few weeks before Kamran's wedding, Hamza offered to organize a party for Kamran. Traditionally there are many, many pre-wedding celebrations before a Muslim marriage like Kamran's.

Hamza was planning a slightly racier type of party — a bachelor party if you will — but nowhere near as raucous or debauched as some Western bachelor parties can be. He told us that a few girls would be coming to dance that evening and that one of them would be Rukhsana. He paid a large sum of money to Rukhsana's "mother" in order for them to agree to travel to Peshawar from Lahore. Three other girls would also be dancing. The event was planned for two days before Kamran's wedding. We were all very excited.

Rukhsana arrived with her adopted mother and her mother's sons (also known as her bodyguards). On the night of the party, everyone had a great time. Rukhsana looked beautiful. Hamza was very happy and Kamran was very grateful to Hamza for organizing a fantastic night of entertainment for all of our friends. The celebration went on into the early hours of the morning and it was about 3:00 a.m. by the time everyone had gone home. Hamza and I both stayed at Kamran's house that night. Rukhsana and her entourage were staying in a house nearby which was rented for this special occasion.

The next morning Kamran woke me up around 9:00 a.m. to tell me that Hamza had left in the night, but not before leaving a note. In the note, Hamza wished Kamran a very happy wedding day and much hope for his future happiness together with his new wife. He also left them 5000 rupees as a wedding gift.

While we were digesting this information, we learned that Rukhsana was also missing. She too had disappeared in the middle of the night. It appeared that Hamza, as he had done so often, "went with the flow." Rather than accept the demands of society and live his life by other people's expectations, he decided to rebel. He didn't want his family to suffer the daily scrutiny and/or humiliation that they would surely suffer if he chose to live with Rukhsana in our community. He and Rukhsana decided to run away and start a life on their own. No one knew where they went. I thought they might have gone to Karachi, the biggest city in Pakistan with a population of over ten million. It would be nearly impossible to trace anyone there. But another part of me thought they might have gone into the mountains to start a new, simple life there. I often wondered how, and where, my old friend was, but I never saw him again.

I did, however, hear from him one last time. About 20 years after I left Pakistan, Hamza got my phone number from my family and he called me. He had recently moved back to Multan to take over the care of the Imambara. I was thrilled to hear from him, and even though more than 20 years had passed, it felt as though no time at all had passed since we had last spoken. He said that he had indeed gone to live in Karachi, where he started a new life with Rukhsana. He was still madly in love with her, and he was very proud that she was his wife. He was also delighted to tell me that they had two children, a boy, and a girl. He seemed to be very happy with his life.

Unfortunately, that was the last conversation we ever had. About two months later my brother told me that Hamza had been murdered by two men on a motorbike. He had been leaving the Imambara when he was shot twice at close range. He died on the spot. It was a very brutal and sad ending to a life that had been so peaceful and that never wished harm to anyone.

Even though I had not lived in Pakistan for quite some time, I was well aware of the ever-increasing fighting between the Sunnis and Shia. No one knew who was responsible for the attacks that were becoming more and more common. Hamza's murder was not atypical. The killers usually attacked while on motorbikes and therefore were hard to identify and/or capture

Learning of Hamza's death made me extremely sad. I thought about the human tragedy and the ignorance of people who propagate hate in the name of religion. I felt deep pain at the loss of my dear friend. Unfortunately, we hear about these types of incidents all too often, but it feels very different when it happens to someone close to you. I often think of Hamza's wife and children and try to make sense of it all. So many beautiful souls have perished due to religious conflicts and differences.

Several centuries ago, the West suffered through a long period of turmoil based on religious persecution. And, of course, religious persecution and hostility still exist worldwide. The West was able to move past most of its harshest religious rebukes through education, enlightenment, and time. The East is still stuck in the dark ages of exploitation by religious fanatics who are propagating hate against their fellow human beings simply on the basis of religious differences. When will it end? When will people like Hamza, who celebrated all religions and loved all people, be able to live in peace without threats, fear, intimidation, or worse?

Chapter 21
When There is a Will, There is a Way

I left Pakistan on April 10, 1988. My friends drove me to the airport in Islamabad, the capital city of Pakistan. None of my family members accompanied me to the airport. The airport is a three-hour drive from Peshawar, and having limited resources, my family did not want the hassle of making a six-hour round-trip journey to the airport and back. None of my family members had ever traveled anywhere away from our hometown, and I don't think they truly believed in what I was doing. Also, and perhaps more importantly, I don't think they wanted to drive all the way to the airport with me because they were not convinced I would even be able to get on the plane. After all, it did take three attempts for me to get a visa.

From a very young age, I was attracted to foreigners in my city. I was curious to know their languages and their cultures. I was very open-minded and free-spirited. I am also restless and easily bored. The desire to travel and look for something more meaningful in life is something I have felt my whole life. I always want to discover the answer to something by myself and I want to make my own judgments about things. I don't want to just read about things in books or watch them in films. I want to actually experience things for myself. I want to see, smell, taste, hear and feel all that life has to offer. These are some of the reasons I wanted to leave Peshawar.

However, I began to really think in earnest about leaving Pakistan soon after finishing medical school. My first job was in the middle of nowhere with no resources. The people I served lived in extreme poverty. They had no money to pay a doctor, so instead, they paid in goods. Anything they happened to have a supply of is how I was paid. Sometimes payment was made by eggs, vegetables or household items.

I felt deep shame in accepting these types of payments. Their limited knowledge and lack of education was also a huge drawback for my job. They expected doctors to know and fix their illnesses after five minutes of consultation, by prescribing the necessary medications without going through any tests or examinations. I had no access to a laboratory or an X-ray machine, and I had no other support. In a country where anyone can buy any medicine (including antibiotics, steroids, and other complex medicines) in a shop without a prescription, my presence as a physician was inconsequential.

Like in most developing countries, the system for getting any type of service was corrupt. For simple things like getting a driver's license or a telephone or electricity connection, (which one might argue is one's right), a person had to either know and/or bribe someone in power. I had none of these connections. And despite being a decent human being, having a good job, and working hard all his life, my father struggled for even our most basic needs. I couldn't see myself living this type of life forever. Thus began my attempt to leave Pakistan for a more meaningful life elsewhere.

My hopes at leaving Pakistan were diminished pretty quickly when my visa request was twice denied. On both occasions, the visa officer asked me why I wanted to travel. I replied that I wanted to see the world. Upon hearing this, the officer didn't even raise his head to look at me. Of course, I had no money of my own, and after looking into my father's finances, the officer refused the visa by stating that I didn't have enough evidence of funding to support my travel plans. I was very disappointed. I was also insulted, humiliated, and depressed by the whole experience. On top of all this, the application process was also very expensive. There were application fees involved, and as the embassies were located in a different city, there were travel and hotel costs as well. After each failed attempt, my father would be mad at me for wasting so much money on my pursuit.

However, I was not willing to give up quite yet. After two failed attempts at obtaining a visa, I stubbornly decided to try again. I was studying for my medical exams and I decided to sign up to take the foreign medical exam as well. This exam was only administered in the United Kingdom. It cost a lot of money for the test, not to mention what it would cost to get there as well as the cost of staying there while taking the exam. Somehow, between borrowing money from my friends, and getting the guts to once again ask my father for money, I was able to raise enough so that I could not be turned away for lack of funds. That, combined with the foreign test I was already signed up for, and the fact that I had found a hostel to stay in, meant it would be harder for the visa officer to turn me down. And, I guess the third time really is the charm. My visa was finally approved. I was finally going to get the chance for some freedom and to see more of the world.

At the airport, I was excited but also nervous about what to expect on the other side. Going through immigration my heart was beating rather fast. I had heard hundreds of stories about how people had been stopped from traveling for hundreds of reasons. I had jumped so many hurdles to get this far, what if all came crumbling down now.

But, at long last, and after having lived in a very religious and conservative society, with few liberties or freedoms, I was sitting on a plane thousands of feet up in the air, thinking about fate and my future. I had no friends, no family, and no relations in that new land, there was no internet, social media, or even cell phones at the time. I was alone in the world, but I was finally on my way.

Chapter 22
All That Glitters Is Not Gold

When one travels, it is impossible to not compare and contrast the place you are visiting with the place you are from. This was no different for me. When I first arrived in London in April of 1988, I was unable to make any real comparisons to Peshawar, but the contrasts were enormous. Peshawar was a dusty, congested city with crumbling houses and an even more crumbling infrastructure. It was a place of chaos and commotion. The bazaars were full of loud people. Everyone talked to everyone else without caring about who might have already been talking. There was no concept of waiting in lines for your turn. People just pushed each other to get to the front without any regard for others who were there before them. Everything was haphazard.

London, on the other hand, was famous for its beautiful, historic, and centuries-old architecture, including stunning houses with lush, green, manicured lawns, but perhaps even more so, they were known for their flawless manners. Most Londoners would never dream of "cutting" into a line or speaking out of turn. London could be loud and chaotic, but there was an underlying sense of order and calmness that I had never felt before.

That was just the beginning of the differences I experienced. In Peshawar, there was both noise and air pollution from the rickshaws, motorbikes, trucks, cars and any other mode of transportation one can imagine. There were no regulations regarding vehicle emissions, so the air was always black with smoke and smog. I did find London to be somewhat damp and foggy, but the air was otherwise fresh and clean. I felt great — physically and mentally — while walking on clean sidewalks and breathing clean air.

London also had fast, clean, and efficient trains and buses, and the roads and sidewalks were free of debris and pollution. I will admit, however, that while I admired the cleanliness and efficiency of the public transit system in London, I was terrified by the silence on the trains. It was so quiet that I was afraid to make even the slightest movement for fear it would disturb the peace. I used to travel to London from the suburbs on an early morning train, and I could not understand how it could be so quiet on such a packed train. People simply looked down at their books or newspapers. No one conversed or even made eye contact with other passengers. It was very strange.

Even comparing what people wore was a fascinating experience. In Peshawar, the men all wore traditional white and brown salwar kameez and the women were covered head to toe in shawls or black burkas. It was a complete culture shock to see young women dressed in beautiful — and shorts! — skirts walking along the streets of London. Londoners wore so many different styles and colors of clothes; it was like a rainbow and I found it to be very liberating. Another interesting thing I noticed after walking around the streets of London for a while was that my shoes were very clean. At home, I needed to clean and polish my shoes almost every day just to try to keep up with the dust and grime that was an everyday part of life. After about 15 minutes of walking down the road, my shoes would be covered in dust. In London, I could go for weeks without needing to clean my shoes.

I was in awe of all that I saw, but there was one major difference in London that I did not like, nor could I understand. There were so many homeless people lying on the streets of London and yet people just passed them by without any concern. For me, this was very odd and sad. In Peshawar, people would stop and inquire if someone was lying on the ground. They would show sympathy and try to provide some assistance. But in London people chose to "mind their own business" and "not get involved". I guess it's possible that because London has an emergency system in place to call for medical assistance, it is easier to not get involved. There was no such thing as 9-1-1 in the Peshawar of my youth, and in a way, I think I am glad of that. It was not uncommon to see total strangers bring food to hungry people or find shelter for homeless people. This was, however, not a common practice in London.

Chapter 23
Culture Shock

Before I was allowed to travel, I was a simple and innocent young man who was brought up in a very conservative world with very different social and cultural values. In other words, I was very naive about the ways of the world. My only exposure to Western culture had been through some reading and meeting a few people who were fortunate enough to travel to my part of the world. There was no internet or social media, so I could really only imagine what life was like in the West.

When I first arrived in London, I was repeatedly shocked by the many cultural differences between the East and the West. It took me a while to understand what was happening around me and how to interact with people in socially acceptable ways. I was amazed to see all the tall and beautiful buildings in London.

My astonishment is difficult to describe when I saw this young girl reading a newspaper sitting on the subway train. She was looking at page 3. At that time the English tabloid newspapers would have a picture of a topless girl on that page. I cannot tell you the shock which went through my mind at that time. I literally held my breath. It was not that I had not seen those pictures before, but the whole situation was shocking for me. I could not believe that she was sitting in the middle of everyone and no one was bothered by this and there was no reaction from her or from anyone else. This was the thing that was beyond my comprehension. Growing up in the most conservative part of the world, where women would be totally covered with burkas, this kind of sight was unimaginable and possession of this type of image in public would put you in jail for a long time.

Everything was new and strange. Seeing young couples holding hands and showing affection in public was totally new, yet refreshing. Back home it was normal for male friends to hold hands in public. In the West, this was regarded as a sign of a homosexual relationship. Drinking alcohol in public was banned in my part of the world, so going to pubs, nightclubs, and parties, where one could freely interact with the opposite sex, was a real eye-opener for me.

I could not believe it when one of my female co-workers, (who was probably romantically interested in me) invited me to go to the countryside with her for the weekend, especially when she said that we would be staying in her aunt's house. In the East, it was impossible for a boy and girl to go out on a date, never mind spend the weekend at a relative's house. That type of adventure in Pakistan would probably end up with someone getting killed. Just a friendly smile from a girl, a sign of being polite in the West, would be regarded as a major come-on in Pakistan, and most people would not regard it as a good thing.

Another time, I was invited to a party by a male friend. There were some girls there, but I did not know them and I was shy and reserved around them.

A bit later, when three more girls walked into the party, I was the only one who stood up and offered my seat to them. Back home, as a courtesy, a male would always offer his seat to a female. The girls were pleasantly surprised by my gesture and wanted to know more about me and my culture. I presume they found it a little odd in a casual party of young people for someone to act so politely.

It took me a long time to find my footing in the West. I stumbled often regarding cultural and social differences, but there was one regrettable incident, in particular, that will forever be lodged in my memory. A few months after my arrival I moved into an apartment with an Irish fellow named Peter. I had also just started my first job as a doctor at a nearby hospital. One evening Peter invited a few of his friends to our apartment. He mentioned that one of his friends, Christine, would also be attending the party. He said that Christine was overweight and it would be nice of me, being a doctor, to discuss her weight issue and to offer her some help. He asked me to check with Christine that evening if she wanted to be enrolled in the weight-loss program at the hospital. As a point of reference, being overweight in my culture was not a big deal. In fact, it was thought to be a sign of prosperity and people talked about weight (their own and others) without reservation.

On the night of the party, while we all were sitting in the family room, Peter discreetly reminded me to bring up this topic with Christine. In my complete innocence and ignorance, and in front of the other guests, I asked Christine about her weight and what she had done to address the issue. I offered to help her enroll in the weight loss program at the hospital. To my surprise the whole room got quiet, and to my horror, I saw tears in Christine's eyes. Then I noticed the slight smile on Peter's face. That night I did not fully understand the degree of hurt I had caused Christine, but looking back, I see that Peter was taking advantage of my innocence and lack of understanding. It took me a long time to realize how naïve I was.

Similarly, there were certain surprises in store for me as I started to practice medicine in the West. I remember my first day seeing patients in London. My third patient of the day was a man in his forties. He came to the clinic with a very bad infection in his ears. I remember him being very polite except for his appearance, especially his clothes, I could guess that he came from a poor socioeconomic background. I chatted with him and then took him to the procedure room to clean his ears of the infection using the microscope. He felt better instantly as I removed all those infected debris from both of his ears. He was very grateful and thanked me multiple times. I still needed to write him a prescription for the ear drops. I gave him the prescription with the instruction to use the medication. I left the room to go back into the procedure room to talk to the nurse about something. As I came back to dictate my clinic notes (we dictated all the notes using a small dictaphone), I could not find my dictaphone. I was not sure what happened and inquired from the nurse. It was interesting to hear her reply to my inquiry as she commented "Welcome to London". I could not have imagined in my wild dreams that the man who I just treated and made a lot better, went away with my dictaphone on his way out. Now that I think of that episode, it gives me an interesting insight into the differences between the two cultures. I would not have expected this kind of response from my patients back home. Usually, poor people back home were simple and would be very grateful to doctors for doing them a favor. Now saying that there were all kinds of crimes in Peshawar but the location and the type of the incident which happened that day took me by surprise.

Another astonishing scenario happened to me as I started to work in the ER in Dublin, Ireland. I was amazed to see many intoxicated people arrive at the ER looking for shelter for the night. This was surprising for me because back home alcohol was banned and we did not see inebriated people. However, there is one particular episode that happens to have stayed with me for many years. A man in his fifties came to the ER due to a head injury. I was expecting a trauma by a fall or an accident but I could not hide my amazement when he told me that his wife hit him on the head with a stiletto heel. That injury left a small depression in the skull bone. While I ordered the necessary tests and investigation, I was shocked by the story. It could not have happened in my wildest dream back home. We would expect injuries to women by men due to a totally male-dominated culture.

I am happy to have personally experienced all of the new things I learned in the West. With the advent of new technologies such as the internet, cell phones, and social media, those types of interactions have changed — for the better and the worse. Before these technological advances, people used to travel long distances to experience new things. The surprise of the "not knowing" was part of the adventure. The Internet has taken away some of those surprises. Now someone sitting in their basement looking at live images of New York's Times Square or London's subway system thinks that they have "seen" those places. But the true experience of a new place isn't just to see it. To truly experience a place one has to see, smell, touch, taste, and feel it. By looking online, people think that they know exactly what is happening, but that is a ridiculous notion. The internet has fostered misunderstandings on both sides of the world. The Eastern culture has been misunderstood by the presumption in the West that all Easterners are fundamentalists and religious fanatics. In turn, Western culture has been dumped on in the East by claiming that no one has family values and that everyone is obsessed with sexual exploits. If a person has traveled to, lived in, or been exposed in some way to another culture, then that person realizes the misconceptions and misunderstandings that can be spread through our new technologies. These misunderstandings are due, in part, to the limited knowledge gained only by seeing the images online and listening to the propaganda. Real knowledge and understanding are only acquired by actually being in that part of the world. I have been so wrong in my presumptions about different things only to realize that my opinions and impressions were based on completely false information.

It took me years to understand and to connect the dots between the different cultural expectations of the

East and the West. It was only by living among and interacting closely with people that I could start to understand the politics, religion, and social customs of a region. In reality, most people in both the East and the West are decent people with good family and social values. Easterners do tend to be more conservative and perhaps more religiously inclined people, but that does not mean they are all fanatics, while Westerners tend to be more liberal and open-minded, but that does not mean they are all loose and without scruples.

Chapter 24
Progress! What Progress?

I arrived in Ireland to start my rotation in the ER department in the fall of 1989. My life in Dublin was simple. I did not have a lot of money but I was content and I felt enriched. As I walked the unfamiliar streets of Dublin I felt liberated and completely relaxed. I would often buy fish and chips from a local shop. The paper covering the fish was soaked with oil but it all tasted so good and it made me really happy. To this day, just the thought of fish and chips takes me back to that happy time in my life. I know that it wasn't only the fish or chips that made me content; it was also my state of mind. Even the most expensive meals, in the fanciest restaurants, have not given me as much joy as the simple everyman meal of fish and chips. I often wonder why something so simple can bring so much pleasure. Thinking back, I know that it was my state of mind which made everything taste better.

I noticed that Irish people in general lived life simply. Farmers, carpenters, mechanics, and shopkeepers all went about their daily routines and led ordinary lives. No one was striving for unattainable things. They simply did what they could to provide a simple but good and happy life for their families. People walked about carefree with no worries. Young people sat in parks holding hands with love in their eyes. Most people went to church and spent time with their families and loved ones. It was such a pleasure to live in that country at that time. There was simplicity and innocence in daily life. There was a sense of calm in the country and yet the laughter in the pubs was palpable and contagious. It didn't hurt that the girls were beautiful, free-spirited, and enjoyed "living for the moment."

As I have grown and matured, and (with the advent of easier travel and access to other countries) the world has seemed to get smaller. I have also noticed that as people get wealthier and more prosperous, the simple pleasures of life no longer make them happy. Happiness becomes more difficult to achieve. Things, like meeting with family members or sitting with friends, or eating together, do not bring as much pleasure anymore. People feel that they have to spend a lot more money in order to achieve those pleasures. I found this phenomenon to be true in Ireland as well as in many places. When the economic boom started, the new wealth of the people and country started to change. The relaxed, slow, and easy pace of life started to fade away especially in big cities. People started to get into the race of making more money, buying more things, and obtaining things that they did not need. The level of stress, anxiety, and depression also started to increase. In many countries people used to live in isolated communities, not bothered by things that were happening in other places. New technologies were giving them access to news and information that was difficult for them to process. I have been fortunate enough to live in a time and place where people did not use tricks, treachery, or betrayal to reach the top in the fastest time. But times have changed. I now have also lived in societies in which there is no sympathy, emotion, or even a pause to realize the harm that has been done to others in the race to the top. Many people will stop at nothing to win even if it means hurting and humiliating other people. Children are now taught the phrase "to get ahead in the game" as soon as they can crawl. I am still trying to figure out what that game is.

Some will argue that when some people succeed it is a boom for all of humanity. Their success helps others to succeed, and so on. It is how the world progresses. The question is: what is progress? If progress includes humiliating others and labeling them as losers, then I am not sure that is what we should be aiming for. How can there be progress without consideration for other people?

For many people the competition to be the best starts in school. From a very young age, biases are created based on a child's intelligence. However, there is often little regard to the differences in the lives of the individual students. Maybe the student's parents are not very educated and therefore are unable (or unwilling) to help them learn at home. Or perhaps the parents simply can't afford tutors for their kids. On the other hand, some parents can afford to give their children the best education that money can buy. By grading kids' schoolwork, and therefore labeling them as best to worst, are we pre-determining their fate?

I fear that the simple emotions of love, kindness, and compassion that are so important for human beings to possess are not being nurtured enough due to the constant demands to get ahead and to be better than others. Pleasure for many people now comes from trampling others and leaving them behind. I have seen so many people suffer from mental illness and need pills to help them sleep. In addition, so many children are in foster care or come from broken families. Is this all in the name of progress? Is this what we call advancement? This is a disaster. Competition is killing people and it is taking away the simple pleasures of life. It is pitting friend against friend, and brother against brother in a race that has no end.

People used to be happy and content with simple things. They did not require constant change. They used to slow down, sit, talk, and chat. Throughout my life, I have known people whose love for others is pure and selfless. They love others for no other reason than we all share this world. They did not learn this in school; it is innate. They just want to be good because they do not know how to be bad. I wish more people could be like them.

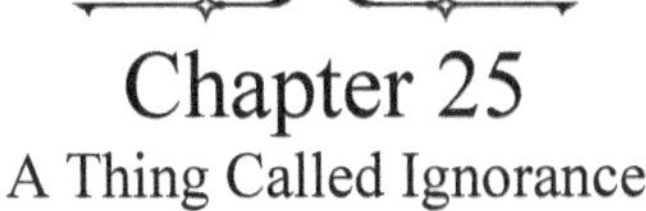

Chapter 25
A Thing Called Ignorance

It seemed like everyone in Dublin had a favorite local pub that they liked to frequent. Their local pubs made them feel comfortable; they liked to be in familiar surroundings and see familiar faces. My favorite pub was a place called Larry's. The owner was a patient of mine, and he and his wife, Ann, both worked in the bar. The pub was not only a place to get a drink; it was a place to meet friends and have a good conversation.

On one particular evening, I was sitting in my usual place at the bar. Ann was chatting with me in between serving other customers, but I was mostly left to my own devices. Sitting at the bar, sipping a drink, in the company of your own thoughts can be quite relaxing and amusing. I was in that state of mind when my friend Patrick came in. Patrick and I worked together. He was in his late twenties, and we both lived near the pub. I was glad to see him. He was an interesting person, and I always enjoyed talking to him. I immediately ordered a drink for him and left my personal thoughts for another time. In Ireland, it was the custom to order a drink for a friend with the expectation that the next round would be on them. It's a good policy — you're sure to get a second drink as well as extend the cordial feeling with friends.

Patrick looked rather glum and was not very chatty that evening. I wasn't sure how to ask him what was wrong; I didn't want to intrude on his personal thoughts. However, the funny thing about sitting in pubs is that after a couple of drinks one can no longer hide their feelings and their tongue gets looser. After about twenty minutes, Patrick started to tell me about his dog, Quinn. He had owned Quinn for about ten years, but he had recently been diagnosed with mouth cancer. Patrick was devastated by the diagnosis. He explained that Quinn was like a member of the family and now he was going to have to say goodbye to him.

I must confess that I was probably not a very good friend to Patrick that night. I listened to him describe his ordeal, but I could not appreciate his true feelings and emotions. In Pakistan, people did not usually have dogs as pets. If someone did own a dog they were generally kept outside the house, and they were mostly used as guard dogs. Growing up, I saw hundreds of stray dogs living on the streets. They barked at everyone passing by, and they often chased after people. Most people (myself included) were afraid of the dogs, and we were particularly afraid of getting bitten by them for fear of getting rabies. In fact, my fear of dogs increased significantly after I took care of a patient with rabies. His death was horrible, and I will never forget his pain and suffering. So, knowing this about me, perhaps you can understand why I was less than sympathetic to Patrick. I just couldn't relate to his sadness. I'm sure he thought I was a jerk.

Fast forward 20 years, and I finally was able to feel Patrick's pain. By then I was married with three children. My wife and kids insisted that we get Lucy, a 3-month old, purebred, golden retriever. Lucy was a great dog. She was gentle and very protective of my children. After my initial fear and anxiety, I slowly got used to her in the house. My kids were very attached to Lucy.

When Lucy was seven years old, she was diagnosed with Lyme Disease. She was quite ill. The vet gave us medicines, but she told us that if Lucy did not get better in two weeks, then she probably would not survive. She did not get better. One evening, we saw her sitting under her favorite tree. Usually, she would greet us with love and affection. When she didn't jump up to greet us we knew that something was seriously wrong. We brought Lucy to the hospital where we were told that she had complete kidney failure and would not live much longer. At that moment, I remembered my night in the pub with Patrick and I finally understood his agony at losing his dog. This was just one of the many occasions where I made presumptions or passed judgment without having had a similar personal experience or without understanding the other person's perspective.

Perhaps it's true that one can never fully understand another person's pain unless they have gone through the same situation. For example, until I had my own children, I could not understand why other people suffered or worried so much when their children were sick. I could *sympathize* when friends complained of sleepless nights while caring for their sick children but I could not *empathize* with them. Once I had kids of my own, I learned exactly how difficult it can be to stay awake all night with your sick kid and then have to go to work the next day. I also used to pass judgment on how people disciplined their misbehaving children. Boy was I wrong. Having my own children, I realized how naive I was in advising them about something with which I had no experience. Luckily, one's opinion about things can change as one grows older, has more life experience, meets more people, and acquires more knowledge. Having kids of my own has even helped me to become a better doctor. My interactions with my patients changed after I had kids. I started to treat kids (and their parents) more gently; I treated them with both sympathy and empathy.

I can go on and on about things where I had to change my opinions. I'm sure all of us have had these experiences. I have learned that without knowing a lot about something, without having the proper knowledge and experience one should be careful passing judgments.

Chapter 26
Irish Connection

Ireland is a beautiful country with a population of about five million people, which if you compare that to the United States, is less than the population of Massachusetts. As a country, it is a peaceful and charming place to live. People are social and friendly on the surface but there is a deeper side to this outward friendliness. Deep inside, they are shy and reserved and they take their time to open up beyond the conversation about the weather, sports, and other chit-chats. It's a country of saints, poets, and mystics. There is a particular mystery to the air as if the souls of the ancient Celtics are roaming through its beautiful countryside.

Summer is a particularly beautiful time in Ireland. The sun doesn't set until about 11:00 p.m., the air is warm and clear, and the countryside is gorgeous. People say that the Irish landscape contains forty shades of green, and on a beautiful summer evening, it is hard to deny that. The flowers are in bloom, and the air is as clean as it can be anywhere in the world.

On one such evening, I walked into a small pub in the town of Bundoran close to the border with Northern Ireland. There was an old fellow sitting in one corner having a pint of Guinness. Guinness is probably the most famous drink in Ireland. It has a black body that appears to be a bit thick and (if it is poured properly) it is topped with a one-inch tall, cream-colored, foamy head. It can be an acquired taste. Some people claim that it is full of iron and is therefore good for you.

As I sat down on one of the bar stools, the old man nodded hello to me. This was the norm in an Irish pub. The pubs are usually old and dark which makes for a cozy and relaxed atmosphere where people can unwind and be sociable. After saying hello to each other, we started to talk about the weather. People always talk about the weather in Ireland because there always is a threat of rain. The weather can go from windy, rainy, sunny, and then back to blustery all in a matter of hours.

After discussing the weather, the conversation then shifted to sports, which, again, was the normal chain of reaction when someone enters a pub. The old man spoke to me about the recent hurling game between counties Cork and Limerick. Hurling is an ancient, and unique game that was invented in Ireland, and is deeply entrenched in Irish culture. It moves at a swift pace and there is a high chance of getting injured. To play, you have to be both physically and mentally fit. Players need the ability to catch and hit the ball at the right speed and at the right time. People are obsessed with hurling in Ireland. During my tenure in Ireland, the country would come to a stand-still to watch the "All Ireland" finals.

The old man spoke to me about it with a passion and love for the game. Being a foreigner, my knowledge of the game was limited. When you are not raised watching or playing the game from a very young age, your ability to understand the finer details and to enjoy the subtle aspects, remains limited. I am sure that my knowledge and love of cricket were akin to his understanding and passion for hurling.

He finally got around to asking me about my family — the trifecta in pub-speak, weather, sports, family. When I told him that my wife was from Ireland, he became more inquisitive and asked for more details. I told him that I fell in love with my wife one night, not unlike this.

I began by telling him that upon my arrival in Ireland, I was "warned" about the charm of the Irish girls. I found the girls to be shy and innocent. There was a certain romanticism to their personalities. As a young man from a conservative culture, I was delighted to be in a place where I could speak with and enjoy the company of women. Then I told him about Sandra.

When I met Sandra, I had been working in Sligo, a city in the west of Ireland. My friend was living in Waterford which is in the South, about a three-hour drive away. He invited me to his house for a weekend get-together. As I walked in, I immediately saw a young lady sitting quietly on the sofa. She was pretty, but there was something else that attracted me to her. The sight of her made me uncomfortable. Usually, I was quite chatty but that evening I was quiet. I can't explain why, but I had a strong urge to know more about her. All my friend could tell me was that she was a friend of his girlfriend.

There was a Bee Gees song playing on the radio, which coincidentally, was one of my favorite songs. I took this as a good sign. As I listened to the music, I became even more aware of Sandra. Without speaking a single word to her, I felt the connection between us then and there. It seemed as though some strange power brought me into the company of my future wife. Perhaps it was the famous Irish mysticism.

Nothing happened between us that night, but on Sunday afternoon, as I was preparing to head back home, my friend asked me to join them for a walk on the beach before I left. If you are at all familiar with Ireland, you know that part of the beauty of that country is that no matter where you are, you are never very far from the ocean. As it was, we were about a 10-minute drive from Dunmore East, a beautiful fishing village close to the city of Waterford. It was that walk that changed my life forever.

So many things in life are out of our control. I was attracted to Sandra the first moment I saw her. As we spent that Sunday evening together, my feelings for her solidified. After our walk, we ended up going for a few drinks. There was a live band playing in the pub and we decided to stay for dinner. The music, the chatter, and the overall atmosphere of the pub transported me to a different world. Time stopped and any worries about my job drifted away. I was simply living in the moment. I forgot all about everything else in my life. My energy was renewed; my senses were awake and alert, and I followed my emotions without interruption or inhibition. As I declared my fondness for Sandra that night, I completely forgot that I had to work the next day. Who could blame me? After all, I was in the process of making one of the most important decisions of my life.

The contrast between Sandra and I could not have been more different. Sandra grew up in an Irish Catholic family with churches and priests. I was brought up in a Muslim family surrounded by mosques and imams. She was brought up in an open culture with Western values of freedom and I was brought up in a very strict and conservative culture. Our values, language, race, and religion were all different. But we were falling in love nonetheless.

This was not the way my life was supposed to unfold. I was supposed to marry someone from my religion, sect, language, and race as well as from a similar economic and social background. Yet, here I was, in the drunkenness of my youth ignoring all of these constraints. I knew from a very young age that I wanted to travel and meet and learn about other people and cultures. I found a similar want in Sandra. She also moved away from home after finishing school, lived in different countries, and had the desire to be free from familial and social obligations. The timing was right, and fate brought us together. We did not think about the biases that had been carved in our brains from a young age. Instead, we acted on instinct. We did what seemed to be natural and followed our own path. We did not want to control the tide, we wanted to flow with it. We also did not care about the opinions of the people around us. After about two years we moved to America and decided to marry to start our family.

Back in the bar in Bundoran, the old man was charmed by my love story and became more open in our conversation. Irish men, in general, need a little more time, and maybe a few more drinks, before they open up to a more in-depth conversation. He slowly started to tell me more about his life. He said that he had lived in America for most of his adult life. As a young man, he worked in the fishing trade on the coast of Galway, an old city in the west of Ireland. He moved to America in his early twenties. He found work as a construction worker in New York as was common among young, Irish immigrants at that time. He worked hard and was ultimately able to establish his own business. He bought old homes and renovated them. Then began buying houses along the Massachusetts coast. This made him very wealthy, but it also meant traveling nonstop. He began to link his happiness and success with making more money and signing even more lucrative property deals. His 14-year marriage failed at this time. He knew he was partly to blame for this because he had become a workaholic obsessed with making more money. Then he told me about a friend of his and how what happened to that man finally made him realize the error of his ways.

His friend was a doctor, and they were very close. The friend was a hard worker who was well-liked and respected in his profession. However, this man was also what one might call an "over-achiever". In addition to his medical practice, he also received a business degree from Harvard. Because of his medical expertise and his business talents, he was eventually promoted to the CEO of the health system in which he worked. A year later he was diagnosed with lung cancer, and six months after that he was dead.

That man's death caused my new friend to reassess his whole life and start making changes. He questioned his own priorities and direction in life. He decided to leave America and the way of life that he pursued there. He moved back to a small town in Ireland to live close to nature. He told me he was happy and content in Ireland.

The man was still feeling the loss of his friend, so I tried to console him by telling him that all humans are different. His friend was probably happy with the lifestyle he chose. Many people thrive in high-stress work environments. It was unfortunate that he died too young, but he did accomplish the things he had set out to do. It reminded me of my friend Rahim who died young, in battle, in Afghanistan. He did not know anything different or better and probably died happy, achieving what he thought was the purpose of his life. Both my friend and his friend had something in common. They both believed in their aim and purpose. When we departed that night I am not sure if he understood or if he agreed with my explanation about his friend, but as is also common in lovely Ireland, we wished each other well.

Chapter 27
It Is Everywhere

I am sad to admit that racism and religious discrimination existed in Peshawar. The Christians and Hindus were minorities who faced some prejudice in a majority Muslim country. I personally did not care about another's religion or beliefs, and I genuinely enjoyed meeting and learning more about the foreigners who visited my city. I did not feel I was better (or worse) than them and I certainly did not feel any bad feelings toward them.

Therefore, I was surprised when I arrived in England to see that some of the locals behaved arrogantly towards foreigners. Most of the immigrants were not a part of mainstream society. They mostly lived together in communities in the suburbs. I was not sure if this was because the English pushed them away, or because they were more comfortable living among their own people who shared their religion, customs, and traditions. It was probably a bit of both.

I was very open-minded and believed that if you have chosen to live in a different country with a different culture, you should be open to accepting the new culture and traditions and try to assimilate and mix in with the larger community. Before arriving in England, I had heard about racism there, but I wanted to keep an open mind and form my own opinion without any pre-bias towards the English people.

My first interaction with racism occurred as I was walking home one day when I came across a young girl of about ten or eleven. As I was crossing the sidewalk, I heard her refer to me as a Paki. At first, I didn't fully understand what she called me. When she repeated it I was stunned. In England, calling someone a Paki is a slur. I was surprised and saddened by this incident. What could I have possibly done to this child for her to call me by a slur? I had never even seen this child before, never mind spoken to her. What was my offense? She has to have learned this behavior from her family. People are not born hating others; it is a learned emotion. This was a moment of awakening for me. Until then I had no personal experience with racism and I was not sure how to react to something like that.

The second time I encountered racism first-hand was at the airport when I was checking in for a flight from London to Ireland. The man behind the counter called me a Paki. He said it very softly and his facial expression remained polite and cordial. But his words were intended to hurt and humiliate me. He had a slight smirk on his face as he watched my reaction. He seemed to be very pleased with himself for making me uncomfortable. I was not sure why someone in that position would feel the need to belittle a passenger. All I could think about was how ignorant that man was. Didn't he understand that it was his ancestors that came to India and through tricks, treachery, and politics worked to keep the people of India oppressed for centuries? His country robbed India of its wealth and then left the country divided and destroyed. If anyone should be degrading someone else, it should be me toward him for what his country did to mine. But I didn't think that way. Instead, I was simply dumbfounded by this encounter. I don't think it's easy for people who have not been through this experience to understand how one feels deep inside when this happens to you. Both encounters left me feeling sad and angry, but these were the only times that I faced racism so openly.

I believed that racism towards Christians in Pakistan was the result of a lack of education and narrow-mindedness. I also thought the people in Western countries were better educated and therefore would not participate in this type of practice. I guess that showed my naïveté in my understanding of how the world works.

I started to become disappointed by the lack of basic decency by some of the people in this educated society. I became more aware of the subtle ways in which people can mask their racist beliefs. Knowing myself and my personality, I knew that I could not continue to live in a country where I would have to endure these insults. It was my life and I wanted to do things my way. Most of the people I encountered were very welcoming, interesting, and decent but in time I realized that England was a more inward-looking country. It wanted to cling to its cultures and traditions. The mainstream did not want to integrate with the rest of the world; therefore, I was not surprised when they voted to leave the European Union.

There are many things I do admire about England: their sense of humor, their insight into the world's complex political problems, their great journalists, their fiery discussions in the House of Commons, their world-famous colleges and universities, their sportsmanship, and their great independent thinkers. I still believe that it is a great and exciting country for a lot of immigrants to live. However, I also believe that all empires eventually decline and that all great things come to end. That time for England may be approaching.

After a few years in England, I began to find myself in a similar mindset as I felt in Peshawar. I started to feel like I was living in a closed, narrow-minded society. I wanted to breathe fresh air, live in open spaces in a bigger country, and see more sunshine. So, I decided to look for some other place to live.

Chapter 28
Which Side Are You On?

After living in Europe for a few years, I began to have an inner battle with myself. The still young and vibrant part of me was in constant conflict with the older, more settled part of me. My younger self was restless, but my older self was relaxed and comfortable. The younger part of me was looking for action and was thirsty for more adventures. The older part of me wanted to settle down, was afraid of change, and did not want to take any more risks. At times this inner turmoil was intense; both sides desperately wanted to win. My more youthful spirit was hoping that, due to its strength, it would win. It was proud, arrogant, and robust. My older mind, however, had experience, knowledge, and understanding. It depended on that to defeat the younger mind. I had daily debates with myself on many different topics and both parts had a very interesting take on different things. They often went something like this.

Old Mind: Have you ever fallen in love?

Young Mind: Yes, I have, and I enjoyed it.

Old Mind: So what happened? Are you still in love or have you lost that feeling?

Young Mind: I am not in love anymore. I lost that feeling a long time ago.

Old Mind: Why?

Young Mind: I fell in love with the wrong person.

Old Mind: Do you think you'll fall in love again?

Young Mind: It's possible; if the right person comes along.

Old Mind: How will you know who the right person is? You made that mistake once before. You think you know what you want but you don't know how to find it. You look at something that your eyes admire but your appreciation is very superficial. You have not built deeper connections and associations in order to determine if something is worth pursuing and if it will last. You have no helpful input from the other centers of the brain that usually become refined and polished over time by reading beautiful pieces of literature, traveling to all the interesting places, listening to fantastic pieces of music, and experiencing so many new things. Those are the centers so critical to help you understand and interpret the visual information about the person that you think you like. You probably think you love a person because the visual center tells you that the sight is pleasing. However, you are naive. Your mind lacks refinement; all the other centers that are needed to help make the right decision are not there to help. You make choices with little knowledge and experience, and so the outcome might be wrong. Your senses need to be refined before you can make an educated decision. These refined senses will make you better equipped to recognize true love when it comes around.

The Young Mind thought for some time and realized that the Old Mind's argument had some merit.

Young Mind: Some of what you say is true. However, you are old. Even if you make the right choice, you don't enjoy the feeling the way I do. You are no longer passionate about your choices or decisions. Your feelings and emotions are weak. My mind is focused on what I want with no distractions from my past. I live in the moment with no inhibitions. You let your inhibitions and fears get in the way. You have scars from all of your previous encounters. You are a coward and that makes you old.

Old Mind sighed and thought about what Young Mind said.

Old Mind: You are mistaken, my young friend. My feelings are deep and are on a different level. I am smart, intelligent, well-read, and well-traveled which makes me polished and refined. I make better choices. You are naive, uncultured, and arrogant. You have no comparison with me.

After listening to this, the young mind could not control himself and shouted:

Young Mind: I am young and healthy. I don't have negative thoughts. I don't have any experience with failure. I don't think of the consequences. I do things because I am not afraid of falling and failing. I am not a coward like you. You are miserable; you overthink everything. Your experiences are your downfall. You do not want to take risks because you overthink and analyze yourself into paralysis. You should not be comparing yourself to me.

Then he started to laugh as he walked away to start his new life in the United States of America

Chapter 29
A Great Country

As I flew into Boston from Dublin in June of 2000, I was thinking of all the people before me who have crossed the oceans and other barriers to reach its shores. Thinking of the native Americans migrating from Siberia to the John Winthrop party of puritans with his dream of a city on a hill [not sure what he would think now} and all the others who have made a home here. I was nervous but excited to start a new life. I was in a unique position to have now lived for a long time in Europe. I was curious to see what this country (blamed by some for its imperialism and admired by others for its nation-building) has to offer to me and how my life would change.

The secret of American innovation and success is in its history and its diversity. America was founded on the notion of freedom for all, and in its relatively short 244 years, it has continued to foster that idea. Some Americans would like to see America close its borders, but in doing so that would ruin the main thing that makes America so wonderful and so unique.

America is new and restless. America is a great nation because of its diversity and because of the open-mindedness and hard work of its citizens. Its generations of immigrants, the openness of its society, its people, and its workforce, combined with its willingness to accept the views and ideas of others has led to its success. The population of most other countries is homogeneous. They are made up mostly of people that were born there and whose families have lived there for centuries. They have become stagnant. In contrast, very few Americans can claim native blood. Instead, there is a constant flow of people from all over the world bringing different cultures, ideas, languages, and talents. America is a great melting pot.

The ever-changing ideals in American society are due to the continuous influx of immigrants and should be the envy of the world. America not only accepts these people, but it also embraces their traditions, customs, and values. American society is dynamic and fluid. America is not a slave to tradition or older customs or values. It is constantly changing. It is adopting all the things from all over the world. It tests the traditions and values which are brought to this country by immigrants from other parts. It checks it. It plays with it. If it is good, it keeps it. Otherwise, it is replaced by other newer traditions, values, or customs. If people eventually get tired of some traditions, they simply move on and create new ones. Because of its wide diversity, America is unique and is the only country that has this ability. People come to America to make a better life for themselves, but, in that process, they also contribute to and change society for the better.

The geography of America has also led to its success. It is a huge landmass that includes many different landscapes and climates; beaches, mountains, lakes, rivers, plains, and deserts are all contained within its borders. In the winter, when it is cold in the north, the sun is shining warm and bright in the south. And while The Rocky Mountains are covered in snow, the sandy California beaches beckon. Americans never need to leave their own country to get a change of scenery or lifestyle. In addition to its landscape (or perhaps because of it), America can boast about never having endured a significant invasion from a foreign adversary. Culturally, politically, and geographically, America is unique.

America is unique in many other ways. America has invented its own sports and has declined to follow the rest of the world's traditions. It has created American football from rugby, which is played all around the world. Similarly, cricket has been changed to baseball. If it cannot change the sport itself, it has decided to change the name of the sports of the world. Soccer has replaced the name of the game which is known as football around the world. All this tells you that we are dealing with a country that is not afraid to break away from the traditions followed by the rest of the world.

Comparing America to the rest of the world is like comparing a child to an old man. Both get exposed to new ideas and technologies. But the child, who has just started their learning processes, adapts more easily to new things. The old man, on the other hand, has reservations about new things. He is set in his ways. It is difficult for him to change because he has always done things a certain way. This is what's happening in the world. America is like a child with a fresh, open mind. Other countries are old and set in their ways. They don't like to change. They are afraid of it. Change is difficult and nobody wants to change the way they do certain things, especially if they have been doing them for centuries.

So let's make the American experiment a universal experiment. The world is becoming more educated, more open, and more global. Decent human beings everywhere understand that the right thing to do is to respect other human beings and to create a society where everyone is respected, treated equally, and gets a fair chance. Hopefully, with new innovations and advancements in travel and communication, it won't be long before the whole world starts to incorporate some of America's ideas and successes into their cultures. Wouldn't it be great if all nations openly shared the American values of freedom, democracy, and social equity? Let's make bridges, not barriers.

Chapter 30
Unexplainable Happenings

Throughout my life, I have had dreams and/or visions in which my sixth sense has given me an indication of future events. The most vivid and remarkable of these occurred just before the birth of each of my three children. Before the birth of my first child, my wife and I were living in Cambridge, Massachusetts. Cambridge is a small, densely populated city that is famous for its lack of parking. We were living in an apartment on the main road. There was no parking garage or street parking. We could only park in front of the building for a few minutes to unload groceries or the like and then we had to drive around to try to find a parking spot. It was an onerous task that we dreaded.

We were understandably excited about the birth of our first child, but we were also nervous. We were new to America, and we did not have any family near us. Because of this, I think I was thinking more, and perhaps worried, about the impending birth. So, about ten days before birth, I had a dream in which I parked my car outside of my apartment building. As I opened the trunk to take out the groceries, I saw a very young boy who I picked up high in the air with my right hand. I didn't think much about it at the time other than to tell my wife that I thought we might be having a boy.

Fast forward a few days and I was sitting at my wife's head in an operating room as she was having a C-section. There was a drape between us and the surgeons in order to block the view of the surgical site. However, I could not believe it when the surgeon removed our baby boy and with his right hand lifted him high into the air so that we could see him over the surgical drape. The move exactly mimicked the action in my dream.

A similar thing happened before our second child was born. About a week before his birth, I had a dream in which I was looking down at a boy who was lying on a small table. This boy was wearing a shirt and tie and had the face of an older person on a very young body. Sure enough, when our second son was born, everyone commented on how "old" he looked. And, interestingly, he does seem to have an old soul.

Finally, about two weeks before the birth of my daughter, our third child, I had another dream. My wife and I were struggling to think of a name for a boy or a girl. Like our first two children, we did not find the sex of the baby. Despite our very best effort, we could not come to any conclusion about the name. Sure enough, my dream settled this matter. A few days before the birth, I dreamt of myself playing with a girl called Sophie who had jet black hair. I told my wife about the dream and predicted correctly that we were having a girl and we named her Sophie.

I don't know why my dreams gave me these indications. All I can guess is that my mind was so excited about and so focused before each birth. Despite having reasonable knowledge of the anatomy and physiology of the human brain, I have no explanation for these three distinct dreams.

Through practicing medicine, I have come to realize that the human mind is incredible and is capable of things we may never fully comprehend. The power of positive thinking is one of those "magical" things. For example, I have seen first-hand the difference between two patients with the same disease. One who has a healthy mind with a positive outlook and who is prepared to face the challenges has a better prognosis and quicker recovery time. The other, with a negative outlook, has probably already lost the battle. Scientific studies have proven that healing and recovery are quicker in patients who have positive thoughts before a surgical procedure. Positive thinking can also turn a bad day into a good day. By controlling one's mind and thoughts into positive ones, the whole experience of living can be more profound, productive, and creative.

A healthy mind can create harmony, peacefulness, and pleasant feelings. On the other hand, a "sick" mind can be the enemy. When used unwisely, the mind can be brutal and unforgiving. If it starts to get out of control, it can lead to misery, death, and destruction. It is not easily tamed. The noises in the head, the cries, the scars, the bad memories, the horrific experiences, don't go away without leaving a mark.

The question is: How does one control his or her mind? I don't know the answer to this, or if there is only one answer. Perhaps it takes a lifetime of training. I continue to ponder how the mind works. I have noticed that the human mind has a vast power that we all underestimate. There are so many mysteries of the human mind that are difficult to comprehend. People like Einstein, Michelangelo, Raphael, and Leonardo Di Vinci, were considered geniuses. There are prodigies of very young children who defy the norm by producing beautiful pieces of music, fantastic works of art, and mind-boggling scientific discoveries that are utterly not possible for a human mind of that young age. They are very accomplished from a very young age and could do things that most "mere mortals" could never do no matter how much training they had. I often wondered if there was a transfer of souls or energy from previous geniuses into new ones. After all, these traits and skills cannot be explained by genetics, hard work, and the environment alone. There has to be some other non-scientific force involved. Some people believe that the human soul leaves the body after it dies, and if we believe in the science that everything is made of matter and matter is not destructible, then it is possible that this matter appeared in the body of these young geniuses via reincarnation. I can think of no other explanation.

Chapter 31
Generation Gap

As I watched my daughter scoring a goal in a very contested soccer game, I could not help reflecting back on my time growing up in Peshawar. I see my daughter growing up playing soccer, lacrosse, and other sports. She competes against the boys and can hold her own against them. I can already see that she will grow up to be a smart, confident, and strong woman. For the most part, I am happy about this, but I also worry that she might lose her natural gentleness, softness, and tenderness — some of the key traits that differentiate males from females.

In the East, some cultures have forced girls from a very young age to hide their faces and their bodies. They are placed behind veils and screens and most of the time are not allowed to make any decisions about their lives, never mind their bodies. However, because they are hiding behind long clothes and veils, they are not bothered by society's judgment of their bodies. On the other hand, Western societies have entirely different traditions and dress codes. Women dress in everything from miniskirts to blue jeans, to business suits and everything in between. Females are liberated from a very young age, and most of them feel comfortable in whatever style of clothes they choose to wear. Women in the West have been given far more choices and opportunities than women in the East. However, in the West, some women are very conscious of their appearance and their body shapes because society is expecting a sort of perfection. If, for example, girls and young women look toward celebrities as a measure of how they should look, this can cause problems such as anxiety and self-shaming if they can't attain the same body type/shape/size as a beloved celebrity. Movies, TV, and magazines, by promoting the culture of beautiful women dressed in pretty clothes, have created false expectations for all women. When I first came to the West, I was surprised that there was so much focus on the physical appearance of women. This type of culture gives young people the impression that physical appearances and outward beauty are important qualities to have.

In both cultures, women are, in some way, trapped. In the East, they are physically trapped behind curtains and veils, and in the West, they are mentally trapped behind what is considered physically desirable. Both societies are narrow-minded in regard to the treatment of women. In the East, they have been persecuted because of strict religious, cultural, and educational restrictions. In the West, people are better educated but they tend to be concerned with more superficial and outward appearances. I don't think women should be judged by their outward appearance but there are interesting cultural differences that I want to point out. Eastern cultures have a long tradition of keeping women inhibited. Eastern women are more protected and reserved. Young girls are usually kept busy with learning to cook, embroider, dance, and appreciate music. They have little, if any, exposure to sports or other physical activities. Women are regarded as the delicate and softer sex. Eastern women are reserved, shy, and passive in nature (Although it's changing). They are usually at home, keeping the house and taking care of children. (they are not choosing to stay home and nurture their families, but instead, in large part because of lack of choice, they are being forced to). The men go to work and are typically the sole providers for the family. Women in the West, particularly in the United States, are confident and want to be equal to men in all pursuits. Along with their partner, they want to provide for their family by working full-time jobs. They are not bothered about the ideals of being soft, tender, and delicate — traits usually associated with the female sex.

I think these traits should be cherished and appreciated because they provide a beautiful and delicate balance to family life and to society in general. The children, when in need of a soft and tender touch, typically go to their mothers. They can also get rough and tough love from their fathers. This is not possible if both parents have similar traits. I have a deep appreciation for my wife. She is responsible for bringing calmness, gentleness, and tenderness into our home. Beauty, charm, gentleness, and tenderness are the qualities of the female sex that hold so much power. If societies don't appreciate or admire these qualities, then that will be their loss. I understand that change is happening and the traits which differentiate the two sexes are disappearing. I am not sure if it's good or bad. I'd love it if my daughter could keep her softer and gentler side as she grows to be an educated and confident woman. I presume that this type of personality will make life more interesting and will be beneficial to her future children and her family. But, who am I to lecture anyone on this issue? My daughter is growing fast and I am a mere bystander watching without much control over the matter.

Chapter 32
The More The Merrier

Have you ever wondered why your enjoyment is more profound when you visit a particular place with your children or a loved one rather than by yourself? Or why does the food taste better and the pleasure of eating is more intense when you are in the company of your family or friends? Why does a song sound much better when it is sung by a beautiful singer?

In our lifetime, we have millions of encounters with thousands of people. We visit lots of places and attend many events. However, only certain events, places, or people leave special impressions in our memory. We can always recall *that* particular encounter or activity no matter how long ago it happened. I believe that it is because many of our senses, not just one, were stimulated at the same time when that event happened.

Human beings are blessed with five amazing and beautiful senses: taste, smell, sight, sound, and touch. All of these fantastic senses enhance our appreciation of the things around us. Sometimes we only use one sense, and other times, we use multiple senses. For example, imagine that you are visiting a garden. While in the garden your sense of sight appreciates the beauty, your sense of smell appreciates the perfume of the blossoms, your sense of sound appreciates the accompanying birdsong, and your sense of touch appreciates the soft petals on the flowers. If you happen to be in a vegetable garden, then your sense of taste may also be rewarded. To top it all off, throw in the company of a loved one, and you've got yourself a recipe for a perfect day that might be imprinted on your soul forever. This interaction of multiple senses wakes up the deeper connections in our brain and arouses the feelings and emotions that lie hidden deep inside us. These rare but special events and encounters are the ones that we remember clearly and vividly forever.

I will mention two such memories that I "visit" often. The first one happened about 25 years ago on a beautiful cricket field in Ireland. I had passed my medical boards the day before and I felt happy and relieved. The sun was out and the air was fresh. The Irish countryside is beautiful when the sun is shining. The sun does not come out that often in that part of the world but when it does, the beautiful, rolling hills, with all of the shades of green, start to dance.

My friends and I were playing our weekly cricket match. At one point I stopped what I was doing and just looked up at the sky. I felt such incredible joy; it was, without a doubt, *the* perfect moment. The whole event lasted less than a minute, but at that moment everything was beautiful and magical. It seemed as though I had been transported into a different dimension; my body felt very light and airy. All of my senses came together in perfect harmony to create that magical moment; I had just passed my exams, I was in a beautiful (and untypically sunny) place, and I was playing a sport that I loved, surrounded by my friends, listening to their laughter. All of my senses were heightened beyond their normal state. If I concentrate, I can still feel all the same emotions I felt that day, and relive that feeling again and again.

More recently, my son was playing the piano and the piece of music he was playing was one that I particularly enjoyed. It also happened that, at the same time, I was reading a book that was very interesting and exciting. My awareness was deep and my mind was fully alert to what I was reading, as well as to what was happening around me. The combination of listening to my favorite music and the intensity of that particular part of the story brought out certain feelings and emotions that made the whole experience better, and therefore the memory was imprinted on my brain. Now, no matter how much time has passed, listening to that particular piece of music always brings out the same intense feelings and emotions in me.

Everyone has memories like this that are remembered more vividly when a trigger — a song or an aroma, perhaps — is released. The trigger helps to keep the memory fresh. Some people call this déjà vu.

As a surgeon, I know about the pathways for the sense of smell. Scents can enter the brain via two paths. The central pathway is through the nose, and the second pathway is through the mouth. After making their way into the nasal cavity, odorant molecules travel to the specialized olfactory mucosa, a small area located in the upper and back part of the nasal cavity. The organization of the olfactory pathways is highly complex and not yet well understood. From there the Information is sent to the primary olfactory cortex in the brain on its way to the thalamus and orbitofrontal cortex where conscious smell perception occurs.

Limbic system by connecting thalamus to amygdala is responsible for emotional component of smell and is the reason why scents are responsible for such strong feelings and take us back to previous experiences.

We don't have clear understanding of the working of the brain but there is complex interaction of the pathways of different senses inside of brain. So, if you want an event to have a long-lasting impact, or if you want to try to remember something forever, make sure that multiple senses are stimulated at the same time. You need a rainbow of emotions and feelings and only then will the event have the possibility of becoming unforgettable. It doesn't happen often, but when it does, it can be magical.

Chapter 33
The Death Sentence

The tumor was in his throat.

Shakespeare said it best when he said, "All the world's a stage, and all the men and women merely players." I thought a lot about my own "Act" as I contemplated how I would tell this young man that he had a very serious and potentially life-threatening disease.

Throughout my medical career, I have heard the most fearful cries, as well as witnessed the most beautiful joy. How is it possible that all of this happens on the same stage? No one knows for sure how their own story will play out. Will it be a tragedy or a comedy? Will they be among the happy ones, or will their act involve agony and despair? Occasionally in one's story, as things are moving along smoothly and everyone and everything is happy and complacent, nature, or the fates, like to toss "unforeseen circumstances" into the story simply for their own amusement. Well, if this is supposed to be a joke, I don't see the humor.

The conversation in my mind was happening at full speed. This always happens when I have important decisions to discuss with my patients whose lives will probably be changed in dramatic or even tragic ways. What advice should I give them? Of course, I would give him my best medical advice and spell out all his options, but there is so much more involved once someone receives a diagnosis like this. It is difficult and painful to discuss the prospect my patient was facing.

Drew and Jennifer were a young, happy couple with two young children. As they sat in my office that day, they wanted me to tell them that Drew, who had a cough he couldn't shake and some trouble swallowing, had a simple illness that required a simple fix. In reality, there was nothing simple about Drew's diagnosis. The tumor was very close to his voice box in a space called the hypopharynx. Treatment options included surgery, followed by radiation and chemotherapy. These options can all have devastating and long-lasting side effects — scars, nausea, vomiting, weight loss, hair loss, possible tracheal tubes, and feeding tubes, etc. But, perhaps most devastatingly, they don't guarantee a cure. The other option was to do nothing and to let Drew live out his remaining time on his terms.

I slowly cleared my throat and told Drew and Jennifer that the biopsy result showed cancer. I also told them there were some enlarged glands in his neck and that cancer has spread from its original source. This meant that the cancer was in an advanced stage and the prognosis was not good. Without treatment, it was a death sentence. This news meant that their lives would never be the same. They will never go back to normal. No matter their decision, their lives were about to change forever.

While I was discussing their options, Drew was looking out the window. I could see from his face that he did not want to talk to me, and who could blame him? Outside the window, life was carrying on. People went about their daily routines without a care in the world. Meanwhile, in my office, Drew's life had taken an inexplicable turn and had come to a screeching halt.

As the news slowly started to sink in, they left my office in tears. They held hands, but I could tell they were both lost in their own thoughts. I imagine that they were both hoping that this was a bad dream and any minute they would wake up. The truth was far more painful. Over the next few days and weeks, each of them would have to contemplate life without Drew in it.

How would the little family move on from such a devastating loss? Who would toss the football around with their boys? Who would teach them how to tie a tie? Who would hug them and love them the way only a Dad can? Everything that Drew created, everyone that he loved, everything that he had — how was it possible that he would simply cease to exist and leave all that behind?

Before I tell you more about Drew, I would like the reader to know my thinking in regards to the human body and the world in which we are all living in.

Chapter 34
The Bigger Picture

The human body is a beautiful, complicated machine. When it is well, it works efficiently and gracefully. The organs such as the brain, heart, lungs, bladder, pancreas, kidneys, and skin, all work together in harmony. The entire human body is made up of trillions of tiny cells, and each of those cells is as complicated as the whole that they create. Each cell breathes, needs nutrients, and removes impurities in order to help keep itself and the body healthy. Every cell and every organ does specialized work and each enjoys the benefits of each other's work. The whole body benefits when each component is working in harmony with the others. Additionally, each cell can recognize its own enemies and provide layers of defense against enemies such as bacterias, viruses, or parasites. The body provides an excellent environment for all its cells and organs to work healthily and happily together. There are common goals and common benefits with common fruits to reap.

By eating properly, breathing fresh air, exercising, and getting enough rest, we provide all the necessary components to maintain a healthy body. But how the body interprets and processes each of those components is very complicated. For example, the body needs sustenance in order to stay healthy, but providing that sustenance is a far more complicated process than simply putting food in one's mouth and chewing. That's the easy part. The first step is to choose to put healthy food in our mouths. Then, while the food is still in the mouth, the saliva that is there helps to break down the food for easier swallowing. Once the food is swallowed, it passes through the esophagus into the stomach where acids help to break it down further. From there it travels through the intestine where it is digested with fluids secreted by organs such as the liver and pancreas. Finally, the nutrients get absorbed into the bloodstream in order to supply strength to the cells and organs, while any waste gets excreted from the body via bowel movements, urine, sweat, and air.

Imagine what happens when one of these things stops working properly or is not available to certain parts of the body. For example, if one arm does not get enough food or does not get enough exercise, it will start to weaken. The muscles will begin to lose their strength; the cells will become damaged. Over time, the muscles, cells, organs, or even whole sections of the body will weaken and begin to die and the whole body will start to crumble. The entire body feels the pain even if it is a small part as little as a small toe. The whole body feels the brunt. Peace and harmony are replaced by disturbance, agony, restlessness, and irritation.

Similarly, in a city or a neighborhood, if there is extreme inequality in wealth and prosperity, with only certain sections of the population benefitting, then the calm and peace of the whole society will be threatened. If there are specific communities that are poor and segregated in the city, then they threaten the prosperity and well-being of the whole city. There will be crimes committed by the poor against the wealthy. If a small part of the city is in chaos, then the entire city is under threat. Under these circumstances, the community cannot live in peace.

For example, if someone lives in a more beautiful part of the city, in a gated community perhaps, but outside of those walls there is poverty and others are suffering, then the wealthy person will ultimately pay the price for this inequality. He or she will not be able to live in their community or in their house peacefully for very long without some consequences. Similar phenomenon happen in regard to the whole world. Countries that are very poor and neglected will create problems and trouble for the whole world and therefore world peace will be in danger.

Now that we understand the bigger picture, I would like the curious reader to understand the fine details.

Chapter 35
The Change in the Soul

Cell division is a normal process used by the body for growth and repair. When there is a defect or a wound due to trauma, the cells multiply and the body heals itself. Once the cells heal that defect, their division stops; they have done their job and the body resumes its regular functions. Normal cells stop dividing when there is no longer a need for more daughter cells. A healthy human body is a beautiful work of art but it changes with neglect and abuse. If there is constant neglect, trauma, lack of nutrition, and/or prolonged abuse, the cells start to change their original configuration. An unknown and dangerous process starts. This process could change the character and the soul of the cell.

All of the information needed to build and maintain an organism — whether it's a human, a bird, or a bacterial cell — is contained in its DNA. DNA molecules are composed of four nucleotides, and these nucleotides are linked together much like the words in a sentence. A nucleotide is composed of three distinct chemical sub-units: a five-carbon sugar molecule, a nitrogen base, and one phosphate group. Together, all of the DNA "sentences" within a cell contain the instructions for building the proteins and other molecules that the cell needs to carry out its daily work.

Each cell in the body has a soul. The soul is preserved by a process of cell growth regulation through the DNA in our chromosomes. There are constant divisions and multiplications of the cells in the body to help with the wear and tear process. There are certain genes called oncogenes that tell the cells to divide and multiply in order to heal or repair what is needed. There are also other genes called suppressor genes. These genes tell the cell to stop dividing when it has done its job. By working together these groups of genes keep the process of cell growth and division in control. However, cancer-causing substances (carcinogens), repeated physical injury, heat, ionizing radiation, lack of oxygen, exposure to alcohol, and exposure to cigarettes can, over time, cause damage to the DNA inside these genes. The damage to the DNA is called a mutation, which is a change in the nucleotide sequence of genomic DNA. The damage in the DNA can result in the formation of new oncogenes or over-expression of normal oncogenes that ultimately cause the cells to continue to multiply. This mutation might cause the cells to reproduce more rapidly and more frequently than their normal counterparts. DNA damage can also result in under-expression or loss of tumor suppressor genes which also results in disrupting the regular aging and death of the cell signaling pathways and leads to immortalizing the cell.

The errors that cause cancer are self-amplifying and compounding. For example, the transformation of a normal cell into cancer is like a chain reaction caused by initial errors that keep compounding into more severe errors, each progressively allowing the cell to escape more controls that limit normal tissue growth. This rebellion-like scenario works against the body's design and enforcement of the order. Cancer cells start to develop traits such as an evasion of aging and normal death, insensitivity to antigrowth signals, continued formation of new blood vessels for feeding, limitless replicative potential, metastasis (the spread to other areas), and evasion of immune destruction.

These changes in genes make cells rebel against the control of the whole body. It is complicated, but it usually starts with one cell, which rebels. The rebellious cell starts to spread its character and its thinking to other cells, thus beginning a process of spreading and taking root in different parts of the body. It plants its seed and roots in other organs until it kills the whole being.

These changes are similar to the changes in a person's soul, spirit, thinking, or behavior due to long-term abuse. Lack of education, poor health, poverty, crime, dictatorship, religious problems, dishonesty, and injustice are common problems. I have seen ghettos in European countries where minorities are kept outside of the mainstream, neglected, and segregated. In poor countries, the young mind is being exploited by religious fanatics as an alternative to having no jobs and no hope for the future. And that's how cancers in societies start. It's not months, years, or decades, but centuries of suffering and pain that are being put on these people. Just as human cells can become damaged by long-time abuse and neglect, so too can societies. Abuse and neglect of certain populations is the start of cancer in society.

Some cancer cells acquire the ability to penetrate the walls of lymphatic or blood vessels, after which they can circulate through the bloodstream to other sites and tissues in the body. This new tumor is known as a metastatic (or secondary) tumor. Metastasis is one of the hallmarks of cancer. When tumor cells metastasize, the new tumor is called a metastatic tumor, and its cells are similar to those in the original or primary tumor. This means that if breast cancer metastasizes to the lungs, the secondary tumor is made up of abnormal breast cells, not of abnormal lung cells. The tumor in the lung is then called metastatic breast cancer, not lung cancer. Metastasis is a critical element in cancer staging systems. It helps to identify treatment options and the long-term prognosis. In the overall stage grouping, metastasis places cancer in Stage IV. This means the possibilities of curative treatment are significantly reduced.

As cancer cells pass their changes on to other cells by way of cell division or by other signals, similarly human beings pass their cancerous thoughts to their offspring, their siblings, their friends, and associates. These drastic changes (i.e., ideologies, beliefs, rumors, fake news, etc.) that affect the others around them will spread into other communities and then to other countries like cancer spreads through the body.

I see the problems in today's world in much the same way that I see cancer in the body. Society can only take so much abuse before it starts to rebel in much the same way the body rebels and forms cancer, that left unchecked can metastasize and destroy everything.

It starts with generations of people who have been exploited, neglected, or otherwise held back in some way. Perhaps they lack access to a good education, adequate health care, or clean drinking water. Or, maybe they live in a high crime area, in extreme poverty, or are simply held hostage by their own government and/or religion. Whatever the case, at some point, they will change and start to rebel against their oppressors which in turn will cause ripples and chain reactions throughout the region and in some cases throughout the world. They, in effect, will create cancer that will need to be addressed, otherwise, it will destroy.

If the abuse/neglect/fear/torment that has caused the unhappiness/unrest/disillusionment is recognized early, it can be removed and the healing can begin. But, if only the symptoms are addressed and not the cause, then cancer will ultimately win. Real change and healing can only come when the abuses and disadvantages have been removed. Making walls, fences, and gated communities to protect the wealthy will not stop the spread of this disease but will only delay the inevitable.

We take preventative measures to protect our bodies against cancer — i.e. wear sunscreen, don't smoke, etc. We should be doing the same within society. Every human should have access to good health care, a good education, freedom, justice, peace, and happiness. These are basic rights that should be adopted worldwide, and we should all be helping each other to gain these rights. The world needs to take care of all of its parts like a whole body, not just some of those.

Chapter 36
Pure Love

It was a beautiful fall afternoon in a small town west of Boston. The late-day sun made the famous New England fall foliage even more dazzling. It was their final display of beauty before they disappeared in the cold New England winter. The high school band was playing, and the cheerleaders were getting the crowd ready. It seemed as though the whole town had gathered to watch the final football game of the season. This was by far the most important event in town, and everybody from small children to grandparents was on hand to cheer on their team. The Hudson High team had just come out of their locker room and like the leaves, their uniforms glittered in the sun. The players were motivated and eager to win their final game and to bring the championship home. They were depending on Drew, a junior, to help them win. His talent and determination earned him the title of quarterback.

Standing 6 feet 2 inches tall with broad shoulders and long arms and with handsome good looks, he certainly had the physique and looked the part of a quarterback. The "fame" could have gone to his head, but Drew was gentle and shy, and he was well respected by his friends and his teammates. Football was his passion.

Even though Drew was a talented sportsman and a gifted athlete, he lacked confidence in himself. That's where his friendship with Emma came in. Emma attracted attention wherever she went. This was not only because she was beautiful, but because she was full of life and was good at everything she did. She was a happy, gentle, and free-spirited young woman who had a lot of love to give and was always ready to help those in need. She had a great soul, and she was good for Drew. She reminded him again and again that he had the ability and the talent to be a great football player. They made a good team.

Drew and Emma started their "romantic" relationship in the eighth grade. They had always been friends and had always been comfortable around each other, but Drew fell in love with Emma one night after watching her perform in a school play. It took Emma a little longer to fall in love with Drew.

Emma was afraid that if they became romantically involved it might ruin their friendship. So, for a while, their relationship remained platonic. However, as the school dance was approaching, everyone was talking about who was going with whom. Girls were thinking about what they would wear and dreaming about who would invite them. Knowing that Emma wanted to keep the status quo surrounding their friendship, it took him a while to get the courage to ask her. But when he finally did ask, she accepted without really thinking about it. She was more excited about simply attending the dance.

On the night of the dance, Emma was, unsurprisingly, the "Belle of the Ball," and Drew was handsome and relaxed. Together they made a beautiful, happy couple. But more importantly, it was on that night, when Drew finally kissed Emma, that she fell in love with him.

In high school Drew and Emma became inseparable. They worked well together and always encouraged each other. That was something Drew desperately needed. Drew's father was always very critical of him. His father was a perfectionist and always expected Drew to do better. This clearly leads to Drew's self-confidence issues.

On the other hand, although Emma's parents were divorced, her mother was very loving and always reassuring. Emma inherited this trait from her mother. She was always there for Drew and helped to bolster his spirits when he was down, and Drew felt great when he was in her presence. She was in love with him and wanted him to succeed and fulfill his dreams. Drew was very fortunate to have her by his side. It was through her encouragement that he tried out for the Hudson High football team, and ultimately, was selected as the quarterback.

Their high school years were fun and happy. Drew became a superstar on campus; everyone in the school knew of him. Together they were the most famous couple in their school. At the start of their senior year, they both started to look at colleges. Drew was given a football scholarship to Virginia Tech and Emma decided to stay in Boston and attend Northeastern. They were happy with each other and in their respective schools. They somehow maintained a long-distance relationship, visiting each other as often as they could. They missed each other terribly when they were apart, but Emma thought that the distance made their bond more secure. They talked on the phone for hours about every detail of their lives. She would ask him about his day. Sharing little details of his life made her feel happy and proud. Whenever she visited him, she would organize his room, his clothes, his books. She made sure that he had everything that he needed.

Once, when Drew was having a bad season and not playing well, he called Emma in a panic. Their team had lost two important games and Drew, as usual, started to blame himself. He started to doubt everything that he was doing. He told her that he wanted to quit the team. He somehow blamed himself for everything that the team did wrong. She could not believe what she was hearing. Despite having an important exam the next morning, she took the first train to Virginia to be with him. She knew how important football was to him. She knew how crucial this decision was for him, and she did not want him to be alone.

He was happy to see her but she could see that he was exhausted. He was not the same Drew she had seen a week ago. She listened to him carefully as he explained his worries. She gave him the hope and confidence that he lacked at that critical moment. She slowly took him out of that deep, dark hole of self-doubt and self-blame that only a soulmate can do. Her love and support made Drew feel better about himself. When Virginia Tech went on to win an important game against Notre Dame, Emma was happy and proud to show his pictures in the newspaper to all her friends.

Drew and Emma continued their long-distance relationship with Emma traveling to Virginia often. It was easier for her to travel to Drew because Drew usually had football games on the weekends. In fact, football games became a big part of their social lives. After every game, they would go out to celebrate with friends. Michael was Drew's roommate and his closest friend. Often Emma and Drew would hang out with Michael and his girlfriend, Jennifer. Michael was on the football team and Jennifer was a business student at Virginia Tech. Her father was a wealthy businessman and a big fan of the Virginia Tech football team.

Emma and Jennifer became friends and they often hung out together when the boys were busy. On one occasion they all spent the weekend together in New York City. It was a great weekend spent with great friends doing fun things together. They were all young with no worries and were living in the moment.

A few weeks later Jennifers' father invited the entire football team and their guests to his home to celebrate the team's winning season. The home was a beautiful country house complete with a small pond and stables on the property. Everybody was having a wonderful time, but Drew was clearly the center of attention and Emma was thrilled to be at his side. A few other girls threw admiring glances towards Drew, but he didn't pay them any attention.

As they began their third year in college Emma was thinking about how nice it would be when Drew was living back in the Boston area full time to work in his parent's construction company. The commuting and long-distance were wearing thin. She was looking forward to the time that they could be together full-time. However, as she was dreaming of the future, she also noticed that Drew seemed to be quieter and was not always available to talk or get together with her for the weekend. On the times when they did get together. Drew was withdrawn and sullen. Emma tried to chalk it up to his busy schedule, but she sensed it was something more than that.

Finally, Emma learned why Drew was so distant. He told her he was going home for the weekend to visit his parents. But when the weekend arrived, Drew never contacted Emma. Confused, she drove to his parent's house to find him. When she arrived she was stunned to see him holding hands with Jennifer.

Emma froze. Drew, who was so close to her, was suddenly millions of miles away. She was trembling as she finally approached them. Jennifer walked away to give them some privacy, but there was nothing left to say. It was over.

Chapter 37
Self-Inflicted Wounds

The human body is made up of mostly water. Water that flows freely can be calm or turbulent depending on its surroundings. It creates waves and currents. Water that is contained and controlled, tends to be smooth and calm. It's like the difference between a raging river and a gentle stream. The river is restless, forceful, and out of control. It has a destructive power. But streams are calm and soothing; They are poetic and lyrical.

After living in Europe for more than a decade, I finally made the move to America. It had been a dream of mine for a long time, and from the very start, I loved it. America really is the land of dreams. However, coming to America was a big change for me, culturally speaking. The way of life is fast and big. In fact, everything about America is big. There are big cars, big houses with big yards, and huge shopping malls supplying everyone with anything they could possibly imagine. Even the food portions are big. And don't even get me started on the number of choices available for everything from soup to nuts.

It took me a couple of years before I really started to understand America. There was a slow but clear awareness of the surroundings. As I learned more about my adopted country and how it works, I began to take a closer look at the people around me — my friends, co-workers, and patients. The one thing they all seemed to have in common was that they were always busy and always in a hurry. I began to wonder what the real price of all this busyness was.

I had noticed a lot of hyperactivity in my pediatric patients, as well as a high level of restlessness and agitation in average, mainstream Americans. In my practice, I have seen many kids that are on medications for hyperactivity and ADHD. I have even seen kids as young as seven on sleeping pills. What are we doing to ourselves that necessitates these drugs in people so young?

Americans are constantly bombarded with noise and action and activities and stuff. Everyone and everything is vying for our attention, and they use every means possible to get it — email, TV, radio, newspaper, billboards, social media, etc. There is no escaping all of the noise and confusion. And as if we weren't already busy enough with normal life responsibilities such as jobs, childcare, aging parents, errands, and maintaining our homes, we throw in all sorts of extra-curricular activities in the hopes that those new activities might bring us some joy and peace. Every minute of our lives is busy. And it seems as though it is even more so for our children. Between school, sports, artistic lessons, tutoring, and part-time jobs, there is no time left in the day for downtime, or, heaven forbid, imagination time. And on the rare occasion that a child does have some time to themselves, they often spend that time playing violent video games or browsing through social media or the internet.

Even places like gyms, bars, or restaurants (where people used to gather to be among friends or like-minded people) have become loud, glaring places with multiple TVs blasting the latest "breaking news." The presence of just one TV can be disruptive to conversation and creativity. Imagine the effect of ten TV screens all showing different things. How much information can a human mind process at once? I would argue that the answer is not much. The advent of the internet, email, social media, and cell phones, as well as the barrage of constant communication and information, has made finding solitude and inner peace almost impossible. It is like being in the middle of a raging river without a lifeline. It seems as though no one has time to listen to their soul anymore. It is important for everyone to take some time every day to appreciate what is around us. We all need to find our own cool and calming stream to stop by and rest our weary minds.

When I lived in Ireland I used to like to go for a leisurely drive on a country road to clear my thoughts and simply listen to some music and enjoy the day. This is not possible in America. There is always someone behind you trying to pass and make you go faster. Americans are in a constant race to go somewhere, to go faster, to do more, to produce more, to achieve more. People have become so used to always being preoccupied with the next task that they don't appreciate the fact that sometimes there is nothing that needs to be done. We are failing to be "in the moment."

This manic desire to be the first and best at everything must certainly come at a price. The more we do, the more we think we should be doing. Our constant desire to be busy takes away our inner peace and tranquility and instead leaves us feeling overwhelmed and exhausted. One might argue that as a society we are smarter, more creative, productive, and successful than ever before, but what is the point if we are too tired or stressed to enjoy it? Perhaps the worst part is that when we are unable to complete our massive to-do lists, we feel like failures. We are literally making ourselves unhappy and unwell. Where does it end?

Some people claim to have the key, but they are simply trying to capitalize on our unhappiness by having us believe that they have the key to our well-being. They sell us potions, or classes, or "lifestyle alternatives," but this is not what we need. How can adding things to our already busy and complicated lives make them simpler? These courses and treatments are only band-aids. They only treat the symptom, not the underlying disease. The only thing that will truly make life simpler is to take a step back and focus on the things that need to be done and the things that make us happy. Period.

Chapter 38
The Fight

Drew decided to fight cancer. He had so much to live for. He agreed to my proposed treatment procedure which involved removing parts of his jaw, tongue, swallow tube, and voice box. It would be a long and complicated surgical procedure followed by a long and complicated recovery. He would not be able to talk for some time following the procedure, and he would, in all likelihood, need further surgeries to improve his voice and to reconstruct his face. The surgery would drastically alter his looks and might also affect his personality. This was a life-changing decision, but if he wanted a chance to live, it was the only option he had.

Before the surgery, we discussed all the possible complications associated with the procedure, including face paralysis, trouble with breathing and swallowing which might result in significant drooling, and changes to his voice. Some of these complications might be long-lasting or permanent. He would also have significant facial scarring which would drastically alter his appearance. During the estimated ten-hour operation he would be placed on a breathing tube — first in his airway, and then in his trachea. He would be given several intravenous lines for fluids and possible blood transfusions, and he would also be given a urinary catheter because of the length of the operation. I would be assisted by a microvascular surgeon who would help me reconstruct his jaw, tongue, and swallow tube, as well as by two resident doctors. The lengthy and, for Drew and Jennifer at least, terrifying list of complications made the procedure all the more daunting. Jennifer was alarmed and scared, but Drew was resolute. He had made up his mind and was not afraid anymore. The only alternative was death, and that was something Drew was not prepared for.

While Drew was getting prepped for surgery, my team and I reviewed his MRI scans for a final check on the extent and location of his tumor. The MRIs usually give me a road map of the anatomy of the neck and help me plan my surgical approach. After carefully and repeatedly checking everything we started to proceed. During the surgical removal of tumors, I am sometimes faced with unexpected challenges. The anatomy of the human neck is very complex. All the important nerves and the major blood vessels are in very close proximity to each other and the tumors usually envelop these structures. There is always the potential for life-threatening bleeding or damage to a vital nerve or structure in the neck. There is no room for error. Also, sometimes it is difficult to know how much tissue to remove. One wants to remove the entire tumor with some normal tissue around the margins in order to have a complete resection, but it is also very important to leave as much of the healthy tissue behind to preserve function and to help with the reconstruction of the vital structures.

As we began Drew's surgery, we immediately noticed that the tumor was advanced. As we proceeded to remove his voice box, his swallow tube, part of his tongue, and some of his jaw bone, I repeatedly asked for frozen sections from a pathologist to know the extent of the tumor. Examining frozen sections allow pathologists to rapidly analyze and diagnose tissue samples while the patient is still in the operating room, allowing the surgeon to make critical decisions about what to remove and what to leave behind.

Drew's tumor was very close to some of his major blood vessels but I carefully resected all the lymph nodes from his neck making sure not to damage his vital blood vessels and nerves. I used a nerve stimulator to check on the important nerves throughout the procedure. After all the pathology reports were clear, my colleague joined us for the reconstructive part of the procedure. We carefully reconstructed his swallow tube, some of his voice box, his tongue, and his jaw bone by taking flaps from the surrounding muscle and by inserting implants to replace the jaw bone.

When completed, the surgery actually took about 13+ hours. It was grueling for everyone involved. I told Jennifer and Drew's parents that the surgery was successful, but I also reminded them that Drew had a long road ahead of him. In addition to recovery, side effects, and future surgeries, Drew might also require radiation and/or chemotherapy depending on the final pathology reports. The initial recovery would probably be the most challenging due to his ability to swallow or speak.

The next few weeks were indeed tough for both Drew and Jennifer. Jennifer was overwhelmed and in shock, not just by the change in Drew's appearance (he had multiple incisions on his face and neck, he had a tracheotomy hole in his neck for breathing, and he had a feeding tube in his nose), but also by the day-to-day demands of caring for someone with such critical wounds and needs. The fact that Drew was unable to communicate in normal ways, compounded Jennifer's frustration, and exhaustion.

Sometimes Jennifer was just plain angry. She began to withdraw and stay in her room for hours. She avoided meeting her friends and felt uncomfortable inviting her friends over because she was embarrassed and uneasy about Drews's appearance and his needs. The independent, handsome, and energetic man she once knew, now seemed to her needy and "damaged." She was finding it hard to accept this reality, which in turn made her uneasy being around him. Drew needed attention and sympathy and Jennifer was not used to giving this.

Chapter 39
A Strange Thing Called Will

Time passed, and Drew started to recover from surgery. However, after looking at the reports of the pathology, it was determined that he would need radiation and possibly chemotherapy treatment. For those treatments, I recommend that he go to Boston to a very specialized cancer unit. There was a slight suspicion that his cancer was spreading to the base of the skull, close to his brain, which could have very serious health implications. Therefore the specialists in Boston would be better prepared to deal with those issues.

Radiation therapy is a type of cancer treatment that uses high doses of radiation to kill cancer cells and shrink tumors. Normal cells typically grow and divide to form new cells but cancer cells grow and divide faster than most normal cells. Radiation works by making small breaks in the DNA inside the cancer cells. These breaks keep cancer cells from multiplying and dividing and cause them to die. Nearby normal cells can also be affected by radiation, but most recover and go back to working the way they should. Radiation therapy is often a local treatment. In most cases, it's aimed at, and effects, only the part of the body being treated.

Chemotherapy, on the other hand, usually exposes the whole body to cancer-fighting drugs. Cancer cells tend to form new cells more quickly than healthy cells, so this makes them a better target for chemotherapy drugs. Unfortunately, the drugs can't tell the difference between healthy cells and cancer cells, so that means normal cells are also damaged along with the cancer cells. This is what causes some of the side effects associated with chemotherapy. Each time chemo is given, the prescriber needs to try to find a balance between killing the cancer cells (in order to cure or control the disease) and sparing the normal cells (to lessen side effects). For Drew, the decision to treat the remainder of the tumor either by radiation or chemotherapy or a combination of the two would be made in consultation with an oncologist in Boston.

It takes both physical and mental strength to battle cancer. When Drew found out his cancer battle was not over, he was both physically and mentally weak. His physical strength was getting better, but it was a long, slow process. Unfortunately, his emotional strength was waning. His diagnosis could have brought even the strongest, most sound person to his knees, but Drew's situation was made worse by Jennifer's inability or unwillingness to help him in his time of need. She had turned out of their marriage just when Drew needed her most.

Every human has two nervous systems that work simultaneously that allow our bodies to react to certain stimuli. The somatic nervous system is associated with the voluntary control of body movements via skeletal muscles. We are in complete control of this system. In other words, we order our muscles to perform certain tasks and through our brain, our bodies comply.

The other system is called the autonomic nervous system. It is a control system that acts largely unconsciously and regulates bodily functions such as heart rate, digestion, respiratory rate, pupillary response, urination, and sexual arousal. This system is the primary mechanism in control of the fight-or-flight response. We don't have control over this system.

In addition to these two known systems, I believe there is a more profound and mysterious system that controls determination and will. In tough battles and struggles, we seek inner strength from this system.

I feared that without Jennifer's help Drew would lose the mental battle. His parents were very supportive and encouraging, but his wife was drifting further and further away. He was lonely and scared and he did not want to go through this fight alone. Without Jennifer's support and affection Drew no longer had the will to go on. He may have been able to summon the physical strength to carry on, but the emotional fight had gone out of him. It has been my experience that when someone stops caring about the battle the battle is usually lost. Drew was involved in one of those battles where his mind was giving up the desire to survive and fight.

Jennifer told Drew that she was too busy to accompany him to Boston for his treatments. Drew was in utter disbelief. Cancer and subsequent surgery did not break his resolve, but the reaction from Jennifer was killing him. His inner voice, which had been telling him to fight and stay strong, was now getting quieter and quieter. Witnessing all of this, I should not have been surprised when Drew told me he would not pursue any further treatment options. He simply did not have the will.

Chapter 40
Unexpected Turn of Events

As a surgeon, I have had many cancer patients who change their minds about how or even whether to fight the disease. Sometimes they fight with all their resolve and other times they weaken and give up hope. Thinking about Drew's situation, I noticed that Jennifer had accompanied him to all of his pre-op appointments, but was only present on a few occasions afterward. And on those occasions, she was withdrawn and showed little interest in his situation. Jennifer was losing interest in Drew as his physical appearance was changing. He was the same person but he was not good-looking anymore. The scars on his face and neck made him look very different. The tracheotomy hole in his neck was not a pleasant sight.

It had been Drew's handsomeness, physical strength, and popularity as a star football player that attracted Jennifer to him. Now she was uncomfortable with a man with scars on his face and who was weak and in need of help and care. She was thinking about all the parties and social events that she used to go to. She did not want to be seen on the arm of a man with a scarred face. She was sure that all her friends would avoid her. She was ashamed of being seen with Drew in public.

Meanwhile, Drew had sadness deep in his soul that was making his already weak body, even weaker. He was sick and tired. The deep sadness, agony, and anger in him were building up and taking a toll on his entire being — body, and soul. And who could blame him? Not only had he been given a horrible diagnosis with a very tough battle ahead, but his wife, who he thought of as his partner and confidant, was abandoning him in his greatest hour of need. About a month after his surgery Jennifer moved out. She said that she was depressed and needed to take care of herself and therefore was unable to also care for Drew. That was the final straw for Drew. As soon as Jennifer left, he lost interest in his treatment and no longer had a desire to live.

When Drew told me he was going to stop treatment, he reminded me of the corpse lying on the table in the dissection hall of my medical school. Looking into Drew's eyes was exactly like looking into the eyes of a dead man. I could no longer see into his soul. He was a shell of a man. Drew may have been in deep despair, but I, on the other hand, was trained and experienced and knew that, with further treatment, his prognosis was very good. It was on my insistence, and a lot of help from his parents, that he agreed to go to Boston to see his oncologist.

His parents took him to Boston. The appointment went well and the doctors explained all the aspects of the treatment along with reassurances that there was an excellent chance that the remainder of the tumor could be taken care of with a combination of radiation and chemotherapy. The doctors noticed Drew's lack of interest in the conversation, so they emphasized the importance of a positive attitude towards the treatment. They told him that the mental strength and resilience of the patient is an extremely important part of the recovery and cancer treatment protocol.

After meeting with the doctors, it was time for Drew to meet the oncology nurse who would be taking care of him during his six weeks of treatment. As he was being led into the unit where he would be getting his treatment, he saw Emma. She was standing in a corner attending to another patient. She did not see him or maybe she didn't recognize him due to his changed appearance. She was older but she was still beautiful.

She was totally engaged with her patient, and as Drew watched her, he had a moment of panic. He hadn't seen her in about 15 years, but suddenly all his past memories of her came flooding back. What he remembered most was how she had been his rock and pillar every time he felt anxious. She was always so thoughtful and encouraging. Then he remembered how badly he treated her and how sad she was the last time he saw her, and he felt deep shame and embarrassment.

Drew wanted to leave that place there and then. He had no desire to face Emma. He did not want her to see him in his miserable state. He tried to run away but he was in a wheelchair and was at the mercy of his parents and the staff who were taking care of him.

Chapter 41
Meeting A (Stranger) Friend

It was the nursing supervisor who woke Drew from his deep thoughts. She gently directed Drew and his parents into a room. While she explained the next few weeks of treatment, Drew's mind was far away. He had already made up his mind not to come back to this unit again. His parents had no idea about the state of his mind; they had not seen Emma.

At that moment, there was a knock on the door, and as the door opened Emma and Drew came face to face for the first time in 15 years. At first sight, Emma did not recognize Drew, but her face paled as the supervisor introduced her to Drew and she made the connection of who he was.

Emma could not speak for some time. It was as if she was dreaming. She had no idea how to react or what to say. Finally, as she realized who he was and what he must have gone through, she came close and gave him a big hug. Tears started to flow from her eyes. She held his hand and tenderly touched him as if to show him how she felt. It was this gentle touch that Drew felt deep inside. It was this touch that he had missed throughout his illness. It was this touch that he needed the most and that reminded him of all the years that he was with Emma. It was this touch that he compared to all the hugs and kisses that he got from Jennifer.

Drew was overwhelmed. Because of the tracheostomy tube, he was unable to speak, but he found he could not even look at Emma. And his parents were of no help. They also had tears in their eyes, while they watched this bittersweet reunion. They had always been very fond of Emma. Everyone in that room knew that there was no better person to take Drew through this next stage of treatment than Emma. She had been his main cheerleader all those years ago, and now she was a professional nurse who prided herself in helping and taking care of cancer patients. Emma didn't ask any personal questions, and without knowing any of Drew's interactions with Jennifer, she decided to take him through this fight, to be there for him, and to do her best to help him beat this cancer.

Drew was also amazed to see how Emma did not seem to be concerned about his altered appearance. It seemed that she did not notice the deep scars on his face and neck, or the many tubes poking in and out of him. However, she did show concern about his mental and emotional strength after learning that he did not want to go through the treatment.

Through her encouragement, Drew did start the treatments. Emma was as caring as she had ever been. She would often sit and talk to him during his treatments. She convinced him that he could beat this cancer. She made him remember the times when he would feel doubt about the next important game and how she always told him how capable he was. It was her who made him laugh. He realized that his facial muscles had forgotten how to laugh and smile. Slowly Emma made sure that his spirit grew stronger.

She spoke to him in a way that made his soul cry. In turn, he wanted desperately to tell her how sorry he was for hurting her all those years ago, but because of the tracheotomy, he was unable to do so.

Gradually, Drew's will and determination came back and his outlook on life was more positive. He began to emerge from those dark feelings, which so commonly makes slaves of us when we are in deep trouble. It also started to occur to Drew that while he did not enjoy the chemo treatments, he did look forward to his weekly meetings with Emma. She cheered him up. Through her caring, gentle way, she made him feel happier and stronger. He began to eat more and improve in other areas, but more than that, his will to live had returned.

However, Emma's professional care of Drew soon came under scrutiny. One day, as Emma walked into Drew's room, she came face to face with Jennifer. In a rare show of support, Jennifer had accompanied Drew to his appointment that day. Both women were shocked to see each other. Jennifer was puzzled to learn that Emma was the nurse taking care of Drew. And for her part, Emma, maintaining a professional relationship, had never asked Drew about his personal life.

Drew's facial expression was blank. He did not acknowledge Emma the way he normally did. Emma was surprised, and maybe a bit hurt, by his reaction. She limited her conversation with Drew and Jennifer and simply performed her medical tasks. An hour later, she was told that another nurse would be taking care of Drew for the remainder of the visit.

The next day the nursing supervisor told her that a formal complaint had been made against her by Jennifer. In her complaint, Jennifer said that she did not think Emma behaved in a professional manner while attending to Drew and she wondered what Emma's intentions were. Pending an investigation, Emma would be transferred to another unit.

Emma was devastated. She could not believe what she was hearing, and she could not believe that Drew would not defend her in this matter. All she wanted was for Drew to beat cancer and to get well. She thought of all the progress that he had made while she was taking care of him and could not believe that her professional intentions had been questioned. She worried that without someone championing him, Drew would fall back into a state of depression. She was sad and disheartened but had no other choice than to leave the unit and not see Drew anymore. That day she went home and, just like 15 years earlier when Drew broke up with her, she spent all evening crying.

Drew was able to finish his last two treatments, but he decided not to go back to Virginia. He stayed in Boston with his parents.

Chapter 42
A Rare Experience

As I have traveled the world, I have grown and matured and observed and learned, and in my observations, I have noticed that most people fit into one of three self-awareness groups. This first is the largest and easiest to obtain. I will call them Group A. For the people in this group material, things are essential and take priority. They aspire to things such as living in a big house, driving an expensive car, and/or wearing fancy clothes.

Once they have achieved a certain comfort level, then they can move on to other things. For example, these people might like to add a little bit of adventure to their lives. Perhaps they will try more "exotic" foods or pursue a new fitness activity. Some might choose to travel. The more curious Group A people might travel to a foreign country in order to see new places and to experience new foods, cultures, and traditions. The less curious might take a domestic beach or lake vacation. While traveling, this group stays in nice hotels and enjoys good food and drinks. After taking trips like this for a few years, some people in this group may start to get bored with this lifestyle and seek different and more adventurous activities. These are Group B people. Group B people do everything that Group A does, but they also prefer a little more adventure in their lives. Perhaps they start to read more or attend a seminar to expand their general knowledge about a certain topic, or they take a more adventurous vacation, but that is as far as it goes. Generally, the people in this group don't have the desire, time, or courage to go further.

The next group - Group C - does everything that Groups A and B do, but they also seek more in-depth knowledge. They step out of their comfort zones to find a deeper, more spiritual way of life. That is not to say it is a religious life. In fact, it is quite the opposite. They want to explore all walks of life, cultures, religions, and they believe that no one way of life or one belief is the true way. They also start to understand that people from different races, cultures, religions, politics, etc., can live together harmoniously.

Group C people ask questions and they aren't afraid to dig deep to find the answers. They tend to explore the mysteries of nature as they become less interested in material things. They are very comfortable in their own skins. These people desire to change society and work for the well-being of all man-kind by building bridges rather than walls. They have no regard for man-made boundaries. They are educated not just with degrees and diplomas from good schools but also in the knowledge of life.

There is one additional group, but very, very few people in this world are truly able to attain this type of lifestyle. This group is Enlightened. They achieve a state of enlightenment by not only attaining knowledge in every way possible but, more importantly, by liberating their souls. This is done by peeling away the layers and layers of biases that we all learn throughout our lives. Through deep introspection, the Enlightened have learned to unlock the doors to their souls and set their spirits free. By using and manipulating all of their senses and by experiencing deep emotions the Enlightened have a greater understanding of themselves and of the world around them. This is not an easy task. It takes years of practice and dedication to truly open one's soul.

The Enlightened understand that no one person or group of people is superior to others. To them, believing that one race or religion is superior to others is a form of hate, and that assuming that the rich are better than the poor is a form of ignorance. As these biases are removed, the people in this group have both a physical and spiritual transformation. Their bodies feel lighter and less encumbered. They do not carry any burdens with them. They are immune to the sensations of pain and pleasure and the concept of life and death has no meaning anymore. They become part of nature, and when this is achieved, their existence becomes immortal.

Enlightenment can be interpreted in many different ways. For me, being enlightened means having the ability to connect with other people's feelings through your feelings. Each human being in this life has limited experiences and limited knowledge. However, the Enlightened have both the right knowledge and the right experiences to come to an understanding that is necessary in order to achieve a higher state of feelings and emotions. In other words, they can feel the pain and suffering of others. For most of us, it is difficult to understand or appreciate someone else's feelings and emotions unless we have been through that situation ourselves. For example, if a person has never had cancer, they can probably *sympathize* with one who has, but they may not be able to *empathize* with them. Similarly, the joys, rewards, and pains of parenthood may not be truly appreciated or understood by someone who does not have children. However, enlightenment gives you a more profound perception of these situations without having that particular prior experience.

I believe that I have met an Enlightened man.

I met Zane when I was in my late thirties and he was in his fifties. He was about six feet tall with a stocky build and long straight black hair. He had deep brown eyes with a slight web of wrinkles in the corners, and prominent cheekbones that did not give away his country of origin or ancestry (most of the time I can guess this quite reliably).

I met him in England at the hospital where I worked. Zane was there to get his blood sugar tested. We started to talk, and as it sometimes happens in life, a casual meeting at the right place and time, and with the right person can turn into something meaningful. There was something in Zane's personality that attracted me to him. Part of the reason could be that he told me he had spent some time in Peshawar.

As we began to meet more often, I found Zane to be a very deep and philosophical person. Over time we became very close friends. Because of his many passions, he had traveled all over the world and had lived in many countries including the United States, China, Japan, Pakistan, Malaysia, Burma, and England. His greatest passion was collecting antiques such as furniture, precious stones, paintings, and rugs, but his main interest was collecting Japanese swords and armor. He was also a physician with an in-depth knowledge of both western and eastern medicine, a talented painter, a musician, and a martial arts expert. We had frequent discussions about life in general and also about deeper philosophical issues.

Zane was fortunate to be a very wealthy man. He lived in a mansion that sat on a beautiful 45-acre country setting. There was a pine-tree ringed lake with a stunning waterfall on the property in which one could fish or go boating. A stone stable was set near a pasture for the horses and in the nearby meadow, one could often see deer grazing. After passing the manager's house on the right, there was a half-mile driveway to reach the main house. The inside of the house was like a museum with a huge entryway with a double-wide mahogany staircase, a library, a billiard room, a massive lounge, and a wine cellar just to name a few of the rooms. Some of the rooms even had "themes" such as Chinese, Japanese, and European depending on what type of arts and antiques Zane had furnished them with.

On one particular evening, he took me to the room where he kept his collection of Japanese swords and samurai costumes. It was a very large room with two big windows covered with thick cream-colored curtains. On the walls hung the portraits of Samurai warriors. All around the room, there were beautiful samurai costumes arranged as though there were actual men sitting inside them. There were about thirty of them in the room. The swords were displayed in a manner as though any one of these "warriors" could grab his sword at any minute. Zane told me that he believed that in his previous life he was one of these warriors and that his collection was not a coincidence. He very purposefully chose the pieces so that, through meditation, he could continue to travel into his past life in the company of these warriors.

The samurai were the warriors of pre-modern Japan. They later made up the ruling military class that eventually became the highest-ranking social caste. Samurai employed a range of weapons such as bows and arrows, spears, and guns, but their main weapon and symbol was the sword. Samurai were supposed to lead their lives according to the ethic code of Bushido — "the way of the warrior". Strongly Confucian in nature, Bushido stressed concepts such as loyalty to one's master, self-discipline, and respectful, ethical behavior. Many samurai were also drawn to the teachings and practices of Zen Buddhism.

Zane told me that he got special energy from the costumes and this room was his favorite place in the entire world. He asked me if I would like to see him dressed in his original costume. When I replied that I would, he got up and slowly walked around the room very intently analyzing all of the costumes. He carefully picked one of the suits and started to put it on. The first thing he put on was the chest shield which was made of iron and leather plates. He then put some plates made of iron around his back and legs and a pair of beautiful, shiny, and colorful gloves that extended to his upper forearm. After attaching bright red shoulder pads, he attached shin guards and some more shiny ornaments to his neck and waist. He then put on his iron helmet before finally choosing one of the most beautiful swords from his collection.

After donning his samurai suit, Zane thoughtfully settled in an antique chair, and he started to look around at the different portraits and costumes in his collection. His manner was calm but very serious as if he was trying to focus his energy. After a few minutes of silence, he asked me to approach him. As I stood in front of him, he held his sword in his right hand, and he picked me high up off the ground in his left hand. To say the least, I was very impressed and amazed by this feat. Zane was in his fifties and was in no way strong enough to lift me up with one hand.

He held me in the air for about five seconds and then he gently brought me down. His hand was shaking but I was amazed at the force in his arm. Later, as we left the room, I asked for an explanation of his sudden strength. He smiled and said that he had visited his previous life for a few moments, but he could not stay there longer.

Over time I learned many different things from Zane. As I reflect on all the different people that I have come across in my life, Zane was one of the most fascinating. He was very fortunate to be educated in the fields of science, art, and culture. He was very well-read with a profound knowledge of music, and expertise in martial arts. He was also well-traveled, but he did not travel as a tourist, rather he immersed himself fully into the culture of whatever place he was in. He had the experience of living among people of different races, cultures, and religions. All this gave him a unique personality. His body and mind connections were in pure harmony and, with time, he was able to achieve intellectual capabilities that allowed him to appreciate nature in a very profound way. This is a rare combination; very few people are able to achieve this state of being. Zane's ideas in relation to religion, reason, humanity, and nature were fascinating.

In my view, there are multiple locks keeping our souls from getting free and liberated. There are keys hidden deep in our souls to open these locks. One needs to search those keys to unlock the barriers to one's soul. There are intense emotions, deeper feelings, and sensations that one needs to experience before one would slowly unlock the locks which have been placed on our souls for a long time. All the sensations in our body of seeing, listening, feelings are tools to unlock these doors. We need to learn how to utilize all our senses which hold the keys to these locks keeping our soul prisoner. We all know that if the locks have been there for years and years, it is not easy to unlock the doors. In order to free our souls, we have to work on it and we have to condition ourselves.

After all this time, I am still struggling to attain the knowledge and skills that Zane had. I would love the ability to understand my patients and their conditions in order to improve their happiness. That would be Enlightening for me.

Chapter 43
Finding the Truth

While living with his parents Drew spent a lot of time thinking about his life with Jennifer. He was trying to make sense of what was happening to him. He finally realized that the whole time that he was with Jennifer, he had been living in a one-dimensional world. Jennifer's family was wealthy, and through their connections, he recalled all the glamorous parties that he and Jennifer had attended and all the wealthy, successful, and famous people they had met. He thought of the laughter and embraces he shared with his friends. However, when he really looked back at those times, he realized that all of those encounters — the friendships, the feelings of love and devotion toward him, the laughter — were all just an illusion. As his cancer changed his appearance and affected his career, all of his so-called friends and acquaintances slowly started to drift away from him. He thought about how superficial those friendships were. Drew didn't have any true, deep connections with any of them. They were all fair-weather friends. It pained him to realize that none of them were looking into their souls or had a desire to find a higher calling in life. No one was interested in real connections or deeper conversations; they were just interested in fun, and the "next big thing."

When Drew really thought about his life pre-cancer, he realized how alone and how lonely he had been. He wondered how it was possible for humans to be so ignorant about what was happening around them. Why couldn't everyone see that we are all hiding behind masks, never revealing our true selves? Because of Drew's illness and the subsequent betrayal from his wife, he was now able to see the people around him with more clarity. He was feeling content and more at peace with himself. He was getting stronger physically and mentally, and something was changing inside him that allowed him to see the truth. He was not afraid of his cancer or even death anymore. He wanted to face the truth.

It was during this time that he knew he needed to make amends to the people he may have hurt. First on the list was Emma. He started by writing a letter to the nurse supervisor explaining how sorry he was about the false accusations that Jennifer made about Emma and that he should have stood up for Emma at the time. He further explained that it was because of Emma's emotional support that he was able to continue with his treatment, and how she was the one who, in the most miserable time of his life, made him happier.

Next, Drew tracked down Emma and arranged to meet her. She was delighted to see him. She knew about the letter he sent to the nurse supervisor, and she did not hold any ill will toward him. He conveyed to her how sad and miserable he felt about how he had treated her in the past. Her eyes were warm and friendly and Drew was dying to ask her if he could see her again. He knew that she was not interested in his looks but that there was a deeper attraction between them. However, because of Jennifer's reaction to his appearance, Drew felt ashamed by his appearance and therefore did not have the courage to ask Emma for more. All the while, though, his soul was crying for her to come back to him. He could not stop thinking about Emma.

During his subsequent conversations with her, he learned that she had never married. She had been living in San Francisco but had recently moved back to Boston. She had had two boyfriends since she and Drew broke up, but she was currently single. The break he was waiting for with Emma finally came during one of his oncology appointments. Emma was once again allowed to work as Drew's nurse and she told his parents to enjoy the day and that she would accompany Drew to all of his appointments that day.

It didn't end with that. Emma started bringing Drew to all of his appointments. Drew was overwhelmed. He could not believe that fate had brought him back to the tender and loving Emma, the person he had left to pursue his superficial life. He saw the same love again in Emma's eyes, that he first saw all those years ago in school. That love did not end even though his appearance had changed. Nor did it end because he was in a wheelchair and was unable to talk. It was not a slave to other people's opinions and was not altered by outward appearances. It was something much more and it was creating a deeper bond between them.

In the months following Drew's chemo and radiation, I performed further surgeries to close his tracheostomy opening and to improve his voice. He started to eat more comfortably and to slowly get his voice back. Emma was always there by his side as he went through all his appointments. It took him about six months to get his strength back. The side-effects of the chemo and radiation were slowly going away, Drew was getting better, and Emma was delighted to see him coming through. She took him out to meet her friends and introduced him to everyone without any reservation regarding his appearance. She openly discussed his battle with cancer and how proud she was about how hard he fought to get well.

Drew and Jennifer were getting divorced and he and Emma planned to marry. How could he not choose Emma as his life partner? After all, she had seen into his soul.

Chapter 44
Is There an End?

One pleasant evening, not too long ago, four young men were enjoying a few pints of Guinness in a pub in Sligo, Ireland. They were having a few laughs and enjoying the fiddler's music, but eventually, the topic came around to the recent conflict in a nearby border-town involving a British army officer and few local young men. This skirmish brought forward some long-held tensions and anxieties in the area. Centuries ago, Ireland came under the control of England. As a result, large numbers of English and Scottish people were encouraged to settle in the north of Ireland. While most of the native Irish were Catholic, most of the settlers were Protestant, and this caused great friction for centuries. At the start of the twentieth century, there was a constant struggle campaign to break the link with Britain. The Protestants (unionists) wanted to separate and be under British rule, while the Catholics (nationalists) wanted the whole of Ireland to remain intact under their own government, not Britain's. On both sides of this argument, a significant number of people used violence in support of their cause. Northern Ireland was officially separated from The Republic of Ireland in 1922, but the conflicts continued for decades.

At about the same time as the border-town conflict in Ireland, soccer fans in London were getting ready for the big game between Liverpool and Chelsea. These two teams are fierce rivals and their supporters are true fanatics in every sense of the word. It is not unusual for supporters of either team to resort to such things as threats, intimidation, and violence to try to scare them away from the games.

While waiting for the game to begin, Matt and George, both huge Chelsea fans, were discussing how to react if their team lost. They hated everything about the Liverpool team, including its supporters. As they were drinking, their hatred for the other team and their supporters was getting worse. After the game, they were planning to meet up with some other friends, all of them Chelsea supporters. They decided that today, regardless of the outcome, would be a perfect day to take revenge on the Liverpool supporters for a fight that they initiated a few months earlier. During that fight, a few of their friends were severely beaten and sustained many serious injuries. Tonight's fight would be brutal —all because of a soccer match.

Meanwhile, in Boston, there was a debate going on about the Black Lives Matter Movement. Some students at Tufts University were debating the new immigration policies and the bad things that had been happening to Blacks in America for centuries. They were talking about the people of color who have been discriminated against and how the white nationalist movement was harassing them and making their lives very insecure.

There seems to be no end to this human tragedy. I was naive in thinking that by leaving the country of my birth, I could leave conflict behind. But no matter where I go there is conflict, whether it be racial, ethnic, cultural, religious, tribal, political, or nationalistic. Even in sport, something that was meant to be an escape from the day-to-day and bring enjoyment to the people is now full of conflict. This behavior of winning at all costs, and the desire for power and dominance is being taught to very young children on playgrounds.

People will always find reasons to either unite themselves in their sameness or divide themselves from their differences. Sometimes these groups form to protest a wrong, but they can also lead to conflict, or worse. People have an innate desire for conflict, and having a common enemy gives them a reason to fight.

The really scary part is that with technological advances, the conflicts have worsened and become more deadly. In the past, men rode horses onto a battlefield and attacked their opponents with their shiny swords. Now they sit in front of computers and remotely guide their weapons of mass destruction to a location thousands of miles away. A child playing outside of his house can watch as a drone appears above him. Before he has a chance to wonder what it is, a powerful bomb has already dropped which will destroy him and all that is around him while also dig a grave for them.

In order to reduce conflicts among humans, society has to consciously grow and evolve, and the way to do this is to properly educate the populace. It is the acquisition of a real education that will defeat these threats. A proper education stems from interactions with people from all walks of life regardless of their religion, color, ethnicity, politics, class, or social standing. Through these interactions, philosophical and intellectual advancements can begin. Media outlets and governments have the responsibility to start this conversation and to invite everyone to the table. The conversations should also occur between a child and his parents, between teachers and students, between spouses, and between friends, families, and neighbors. An open dialogue is necessary in order to remove the biases that take root in our brains from a very young age.

Dopamine is an organic chemical that is commonly associated with the "pleasure system" in the brain. It is released during pleasurable activities and prompts us to continue to do or to seek out the enjoyable activity or occupation. Rewarding experiences such as food, sex, drug abuse, a runner's high, or looking at a piece of artwork are just some of the triggers of a dopamine release that have been with humans for millions of years. No one needs to be trained to enjoy these particular things; they are innate stimuli that we are born with. We can, however, train our brains to reject certain stimuli as pleasurable. For example, we could train our pleasure centers to not enjoy the sight of someone getting pummeled in a boxing match, or seeing our team defeat another, or by wars or the destruction of other countries or cultures.

Pleasure centers should be trained to enjoy the images of helping and building up other people's lives. This will require extensive training of the mind and of the being. It is not possible to do in one generation. It will require hard work, dedication, and awareness through multiple generations. It will require a "Conscious Evolution" of the human soul and spirit. It will require changing the physiology of the brain's pleasure-seeking behavior with things that bring positivity to the lives of everyone. It will require real education.

Chapter 45
Everyone Needs a House With a Good Foundation

My middle son was playing with Legos. He was attempting to make a house from all these small pieces. He was meticulously connecting the pieces, and gradually the house was taking its shape. However, part of it would occasionally break off, or there were small defects in the design that didn't allow the house to sit properly. My son tried to fix each of these small imbalances as they happened, but he didn't have true success until he realized that the pillars for the foundation were not in the right place. Once he discovered this he was able to go back, correct the mistake, and then the whole structure took shape and stood on its own without toppling over.

Just like building a house (whether it be made of Legos or steel and wood), a real and proper education needs to start with a solid and robust foundation. If the pillars are weak or are in the wrong place, the entire structure will be faulty and will not be stable or safe. The pillars for building a strong, intellectual, sophisticated, and aware persona are created from a very young age, so it is very important that this be done right. A strong foundation in a person can only be achieved with the right education that includes learning things such as science, math, languages, art, music, and history. In addition, and perhaps more importantly, a child should be taught to have a good moral compass.

In the field of medicine, the first rule is to do no harm. This should be the guiding principle for the educational system as well. One should be able to establish a business, make money, become wealthy but also make sure that by his or her actions no other person becomes poor or suffers or is in any way harmed. For young children to grow and to be a successful human being, it is not enough to be prosperous in a materialistic way, but also to have the wisdom to differentiate between good and bad, and to do the right thing for themselves, for their family and for society in general. A few years ago, my daughter told me about a boy named Simon in her third-grade class that she thought was very smart. I asked her why she thought that. This is what she said:

Sophie: Simon told me that he was going to buy all of the gumballs from the machine at school.

Me: How does that make him smart?

Sophie: He said he would sell them to our friends for $1 each, but he only paid $.25 for each one.

Me: Oh, so he will make a profit.

Sophie: Yes and that means he is smart. He will make a lot of money.

Me: Do you think that will make him smart or unfair?

Sophie: I think it makes him smart because he will have a lot more money than he had before.

This was a simple conversation but my mind started to reflect deeply on this concept. In a simplistic way, I tried to explain to my daughter that he was exploiting other kids who didn't know the real value of the gumballs and that he was taking advantage of their ignorance.

In today's society, this is how many businesses are run. Many businesses make huge profits by hiring people at low wages in poor countries to make richer people's products. Their products are in high demand so that is how they can get away with exploiting both the people who are making the product and the people who are buying the product. In this process, they become very wealthy. We call these people smart. Meanwhile, people such as firefighters, teachers, doctors, carpenters, and mechanics are providing necessary services to the community at a fair price. So to me, the kid making a quick buck by altering the supply and demand chain of a product to his classmates is not an indication of being smart but an indication of being unfair and unjust. Children should not be taught this concept, but it is a socially acceptable concept, nonetheless, and not only are children learning it at a young age but it is also taught in the world's most prestigious business schools.

Some companies continue to make huge amounts of money by selling products such as sugary drinks, cigarettes, alcohol, and video games without any consideration for the harm it might cause society. It makes one wonder: Are businesses that make guns and missiles and other weapons of war secretly hoping for more wars in order to benefit from them?

Real education doesn't just happen inside a classroom, it is acquired throughout life in various ways in the home, at school, at playgrounds, and in places like the library or mall, or by interactions with other people. It does not come through memorizing facts or passing exams and getting good grades. It comes by watching our parents and members of the family, and through interactions with friends and teachers, and by learning practical life skills. Children should attend schools that not only provide them with the knowledge of science, history, music, and other "basic" subjects but also with the practical skills necessary to fully succeed in today's society. For example, in addition to their regular classes, children should learn to cook, clean, garden, fix basic appliances, balance their bank accounts, and do simple house maintenance chores. These are practical skills which I think are very important for the human mind to grasp earlier before it becomes too specialized as the school usually likes them to be. This type of education also allows children to interact and converse with a variety of people from all different backgrounds. Skills to communicate and interact with people who do not have the same background or level of education is one of the most important parts of the education.

Providing children with a well-rounded education gives them the tools to find the right path in life and avoid being manipulated by the lies and falsehoods surrounding us all. The technology that we all rely on has made it harder to find the real truth in life, but a well-educated person will have the necessary tools available to overcome these pitfalls. So, educating someone properly is the key to their success as well as to the success of society in general — it creates a strong foundation.

So to educate someone properly is the key to the success of him or her, their family, and society in general. We should understand that real education makes pillars and foundations for a person who provides the support and foundation for the entire society. This society will provide support and prosperity to other societies or cultures which are struggling, and this would result in global peace and prosperity for everyone.

Chapter 46
Real Education

People who are educated properly and have knowledge can live a beautiful life full of pleasures and delights. Their experiences are more profound and, in every respect, their life is more fulfilling. For instance, someone who enjoys looking at art and also enjoys listening to music can combine the two to further enhance their pleasure. Similarly, someone standing among the ruins of ancient Rome or visiting the temples in Greece will have an entirely different experience if he or she understands the culture, traditions, and history of those old civilizations. Without knowing about the Greek gods, one would only see old stones while standing among the ruins of the ancient Greek temples. However, prior knowledge of Apollo or Zeus can only enhance the experience of a visit to the temples. Understanding Greek mythology allows the visitor to be transported back in time and they might even feel the presence of the ancient Greek warriors. While standing inside the Colosseum in Rome, one might only see the stone walls and steps of the building, but if they know the history of the place, they can visualize the battles among the gladiators and imagine the cheers of the crowd filling the stadium. Powerful emotions may also be felt if one knows that Nero burned this magnificent city. Most people can appreciate the exquisite beauty of the Taj Mahal and can marvel at its flawless architecture, but without knowing why or for whom it was built, will not allow the viewer to feel the full range of emotions of deep love and loss that one should feel when seeing it.

Nature has provided us with all these wonderful tools in the form of our five senses to enjoy and experience daily life and its events. In science and medicine, we know only the superficial anatomical and physiological interactions of our senses. What we don't know is the depth of the pathways each sense has in the brain nor the complexity of the interaction among these five senses.

When our senses are polished, the interaction among the different senses occurs at a much deeper level, which in turn stimulates the brain differently than in someone whose senses are not polished and cannot appreciate the finer details.

For example, we know that a person who has prior knowledge of a particular painting and/or artist, can appreciate the minute details and enjoy looking at the painting more than someone who does not have prior knowledge. His or her experience is more intense and more pleasurable. Similarly, a person that has a knowledge of the fine details of music might have a more pleasurable experience while listening to a particular piece of music than someone who has no musical background. If both of these refined and polished senses are excited at the same time, the deeper connections of these two senses inside the brain can arouse entirely different sensations and emotions than in someone who doesn't have the same knowledge of music and art. So, a person that is well educated and can appreciate both music and art, will experience a much deeper feeling about both art and music because his brain has been stimulated more deeply.

Without a proper foundation, you cannot build a strong and beautiful house. The foundation is built early in life but the refinement of the senses is a lifelong process. It continues throughout life as we build on our previous knowledge to continue to refine our senses so that our understanding of everything around us becomes more profound. When our senses are polished and refined, our pleasures are enhanced by everything that we encounter, and we live our lives at a higher state of awareness. But without having prior knowledge of subjects such as art, culture, music, history, mathematics, and science, one cannot refine the senses. Nature has provided us the tools to enhance our appreciation for our surroundings, our experiences, and our interactions, but we have to be smart enough to benefit from them.

So a real or complete education should be designed to build on the earlier foundation, the pillars of a beautiful and fulfilling life, by educating the young mind towards refining and polishing all the senses. We have to use the tools provided to us by nature, and we have to polish those tools and use them effectively to get the best experience and the most pleasure. This is why early education is so important. It forms the foundation for which all the other things we learn in life must rest.

Chapter 47
The Remedy

The human body and the world are similar in behavior. Any injury or insult to any part of the body ultimately effects the whole body. This is also true for the whole world. Neither the body nor the world is immune from trauma. In much the same way the parts of the body are connected, so is the whole world. For example, if your foot hurts, walking and other basic functions of the human body become more difficult and other parts of the body — the legs, torso, etc., need to compensate to make up for the sore foot. In the world, if one country is in turmoil, the whole world feels the repercussions. If these traumas or turmoils are ignored in either the body or the world, chaos will ensue. We are all connected no matter where we are in the world relative to one another.

With cancer, there are multiple factors that are responsible for damaging the DNA of the cell that starts the process of a healthy cell turning into cancer. The good news is that there are multiple approaches to fix this terrible disease such as surgery, chemotherapy, radiotherapy, and hormone therapy. Similarly, the factors that change the soul of human beings — poverty, neglect, religious fundamentalism, lack of education, etc., — also needed to be addressed in multiple ways. Surgery can excise and remove cancerous tumors, but surgery alone rarely cures the body.

In times of war, the invading country is, in essence, surgically removing the immediate threat or things that started the problem. However, even if the invaders kill their "enemy" they still won't succeed in removing all the things that led to the unrest. The invaders will still need to "fix the system," by providing the basic needs of education, healthcare, social security, and other basic human needs to prevent the spread and recurrence of the problems that started cancer in the first place.

We know that when a body part is surgically removed it can effect the person's quality of life but, he or she can survive and thrive with some adjustments to their normal routines. I see this as similar to the wealthy of the world (people, cities, countries) sharing some of their wealth and comforts with the poor people of the world. Imagine that if every person (and/or place) of means did without once in a while on the luxuries of life — expensive cars, bigger houses, fancy meals — and instead, funneled some of those resources to the people and places that are lacking in the most basic needs, we could help to heal the cancerous tumors growing in our societies.

Disaster can be prevented in both bodies and minds simply by recognizing the causes of cancer. If we work to remove and repair the decades and centuries of insults and abuse, then the vicious cycle of violence and extremism can be broken. Human beings all over the world need and deserve dignity and respect. These can be achieved by providing education and enlightenment, by building bridges, not barriers. They cannot be fixed by creating wars and providing weapons. We know there are no barriers that can stop the spread of cancer, only bridges can prevent it from developing into one.

We, as civilized societies, living in the wealthiest nations, have a responsibility to prevent and recognize this phenomenon. For the sake of our children and grandchildren, we should find the causes of, and address the symptoms of the ailing world, and fix them before they reach us. If we believe that *our* children need good food, a good education, a safe and happy place to live, then consider the same for *all* of the children of the world. Recognizing real love and separating it from superficial and materialistic beings is a life-changing experience. Giving and sharing wealth gives pleasure in knowing that we are helping people in need.

A year had passed since I last saw Drew. He arrived for his routine check-up with his wife Emma. His scars had healed very nicely and he seemed very happy. Drew told me that he was able to eat well without any discomfort and that his voice had improved greatly. Upon examining him I could see no trace of a tumor or any other problems.

He was sitting across from me as I gave him the all-clear. I could see the relief and happiness on his face. We looked deeply into each other's eyes and I suddenly felt the connection that had been missing in our previous meetings. I saw what I was looking for; I could see his soul. As we made that connection, I remembered the day back in medical school when I was standing in the dissection hall looking at the dead body whose eyes were cold and soulless. I could do nothing for that man on the dissection table, but in Drew's eyes, I saw happiness and joy. It seemed that our souls were talking and at that moment, in Drew's eyes, I found the purpose of my life. I felt peace in my own soul.

I thought of Karim and of his purpose, which was probably fulfilled by fighting the Russians defending his country. I also thought of Hamza and his purpose which was fulfilled by taking Rukhsana out of her life of misery. While my own mind was going through these thoughts, I could see Drew and Emma holding hands and looking very comfortable together. Their deeper beings were in sync and their physical bodies were in harmony. They looked like they shared the same soul. I saw pure love.

Drew was cured of his cancer and I was happy to have played my part in his success. We all have lives to live and are here for different reasons. Ultimately, the curtain will fall for each of us, but I was happy to know that Drew's life will go on and he will have more time to act in his own play.

Chapter 48
Full Circle

I woke up to the bright morning sunshine and opened the door to the front porch of my house. The bright sun on the snow-covered mountains was a beautiful sight. The hills were pure white as far as I could see. I stretched my arms and looked around at my surroundings. I was surrounded by nature — tall pine trees and high cliffs. I was alone and I was in a state of complete peace and harmony. My body was as light as a feather and my thoughts were as pure as the river in the distance. I had no desires, nor did I have any worries. I felt happy and peaceful.

All of the distractions in my life were gone. Tranquility and inner peace had returned. Calmness replaced the restlessness that had once defined me. Joy had replaced the anxiety. My body was listening to my soul as it noticed the different colors in the sky. My eyes followed the movement of the clouds as well as the shadows made by the sun. I was feeling the fresh breeze on my skin and listening to the birds singing while inhaling the scent of the flowers, trees and earth. Everything that I saw and felt was leaving an imprint deep in my soul.

All my senses were in harmony. My soul was clean and bright; all the scars and stains associated with growing up were gone. Time stood still. It was bliss.

I was in the Himalayan Mountains, five thousand feet above sea level, in Gilgit, a city in the northern region of Pakistan. The city is located in a broad valley near the confluence of the Gilgit and Hunza Rivers in the Karakoram Mountain range. I was about two hundred miles from the city of Peshawar where I was born.

As I saw the tall majestic Himalayan Mountains surrounding me, I felt my physical body leaving me as I became insignificant in relation to the mighty nature surrounding me. With that sensation, I became a part of nature.

This was the state of mind I found myself in when I woke up from my dream. I took a deep breath and realized that nature had provided me a glimpse into my future. Some of my dreams have become reality in the past, so I have reason to hope that this dream will one day come true for me as well. Perhaps this dream provided me with an insight into my final act on this stage. Only time will tell...

Author's Note:

This book describes my experiences while living and travelling through different countries. It reflects my opinions on these experiences. While writing this book, I researched and borrowed information from numerous online articles and websites, including but not limited to Wikipedia, history of Peshawar, mujra dance, hippy trail and etiology of Cancer.

About the Author

S. Kamil is by profession, a surgeon, trained in Europe and the United States. He was born and raised in Peshawar, Pakistan, but has lived and practiced medicine on three different continents. He is a father of three children. He has the unique and fortunate experience to live among people of many different cultures which gave him the desire to undertake the journey of self-reflection and soul searching.